More comic Sense

by Nancy Mucklow

illustrations by Nancy Mucklow

Michael Grass House

More Comic Sense

 Michael Grass House
Kingston, Ontario Canada K7M2W2

Copyright © 2011 by Nancy Mucklow
Cover design by Belinda McGee
Illustrations by Nancy Mucklow

The information in this book is true and complete to the best of our knowledge.
More Comic Sense is not intended to replace professional occupational therapy or professional diagnosis or advice. The contents are not medical, legal, technical, or therapeutic advice and must not be construed as such. Readers should not use this information to diagnose or treat social communication disabilities without consulting a qualified professional. All descriptions, recommendations, and activity suggestions are made without guarantee on the part of the author. The author disclaims any liability in connection with the use of this information.

ISBN - 978-0-9811439-6-5 1. Social skills training 2. ADHD, treatments 3. Asperger syndrome, treatments

INTRODUCTION
What is common sense?

"It's nuts!" Lisa muttered. "People just
expect you to know things!"

"Like what?" her friend Mike asked.

"Those two teachers were talking about their computer problems. So I very nicely walked over and gave them some advice."

Mike winced. "People don't like getting advice until they ask for it."

"See? Now how was I supposed to know that?"

"They probably just expected you to know because everybody hates being bossed around. And they probably gave you some body language signals that you were being inappropriate. Did you notice anything?"

"No." Lisa sighed. "I was too busy telling them how to fix their computers."

What is common sense?

If you've read *Comic Sense*, then you have a basic idea what common sense is. *More Comic Sense* picks up where *Comic Sense* left off, providing new, advanced ways to think about common sense.

Most people can't explain common sense because (they say) it's all about *unwritten rules*. This might make you feel as if you don't have a chance at figuring them out. But relax, the most important rules are all written down. They're called *manners and etiquette*, and you can buy a good book on this topic from any bookstore.

Here are the basic ideas of common sense that were explained in *Comic Sense*:

1. Being aware

Common sense starts with listening and observing, especially in social situations or dangerous situations. Don't let your attention wander. Look for signs and signals from others that tell you you're doing the right (or wrong) thing.

What to be aware of:

- *Who's talking and what he/she's saying*
- *Who's listening and who's nearby*
- *What's happening and what's about to happen*
- *What's moving or is about to move*
- *Who's communicating with body language, voice, expressions, choices, and attitudes*

2. Knowing what people assume and expect

People believe you know what they know and see what they see. Since they learned social rules when they were children, they assume that you did too. So when you do something unexpected, they assume you're doing it on purpose.

People also expect you to do (and say) things for the good of others, not just for yourself. These expectations aren't entirely invisible, because people communicate them with their face, voice, and body language—and sometimes they just tell you.

People assume

... that you know what they know.

If you do something unexpected, they assume you're doing it on purpose.

People expect

... that you'll put courtesy and consideration of others first.

Otherwise you communicate that you're self-centered.

What people assume and expect:

- *That you know the social rules they know*
- *That you're watching their body language for silent communication*
- *That you're thinking about safety*
- *That you're aware what your body language is communicating*

 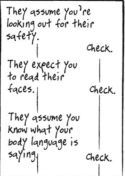  

Assumptions and Expectations

Situation	Assumption or Expectation
You and several acquaintances are walking on a delicate hanging bridge over a ravine. They get angry when you start bouncing the bridge. Why?	They assume that you'll take every precaution for their safety.
Your friend gets angry with you because you didn't notice her silent signals that she wanted to go home. Why?	She expects _____
You ate a lot and talked a lot at a party. Later, your friend tells you you're a pig and a conversation hog. Why?	He assumes _____

See page 195 for suggested answers to quiz boxes.

You can predict

1 **Think about where you're headed.**
   Present events create future events.

2 **Avoid problems by changing what you're doing.**
   Make decisions now to avoid trouble later.

4. Predicting

Common sense means predicting what's likely to happen, based on what's going on right now. It means looking ahead to avoid problems.

How to predict:

■ *Think about where you're headed.*

■ *Consider how what's happening now will affect what will happen soon.*

■ *Change what you're doing if you're headed toward a bad outcome.*

5. Prioritizing

Common sense means ranking things in your head according to how important they are. Tackle the most important things first.

How to prioritize:

- ■ *Do things for safety before anything else.*

- ■ *Do things that you have to do before things that you want to do.*

- ■ *Do things for others before doing things for yourself.*

- ■ *Do things that make a big difference before things that make a small difference.*

You can prioritize

1 Important, safety-related, and time-sensitive things.
...come before...

2 Trivial and self-centered things.

Which Comes First?

_2_ I need to take good care of my car.

_1_ I need to take good care of this car I borrowed from my mom.

. . . .

____ I need to clean my office.

____ I need to finish the report before the deadline.

. . . .

____ I need to get the children away from the fire pit.

____ I need to start cooking the burgers. Everyone's hungry!

. . . .

____ I need to spend some money on a dentist check-up.

____ I need to spend some money on clothes.

. . . .

____ I need to get exercise.

____ I need to catch up on my TV shows.

What to do

1 **Take responsibility for your actions.**
  Fix problems.

2 **Observe others.**
  Do what they do.

3 **Ask for help.**
  Learn for the next time.

6. Knowing what to do

Common sense also involves taking action. Standing bewildered on the sidelines while something happens isn't helpful to you or anyone else.

What you can do:

■ *Take responsibility by cleaning up messes you make, apologizing and making amends, or fixing what you broke.*

■ *When in doubt, observe friends you respect, and do what they do.*

■ *If you can't decide what to do, ask for help.*

Summary

Common sense is a skill you can learn. It includes:

■ **being aware.** Always think about and observe your situation.

■ **knowing what people assume and expect.** Learn to observe their body language.

■ **knowing how to predict.** Practice thinking about what will happen next.

■ **knowing how to prioritize.** Do important things first.

■ **taking action.** Don't just stand there.

CHAPTER 1
More Context

"It's a fancy restaurant," Lily's mom

said as she came down the stairs. "Not your usual burger joint. Just be aware of that."

Lily nodded and quietly slipped her ear-buds in place so she could listen to her music. It was her great-aunt's birthday, so they were all going out to a seafood restaurant. It took forever to find something on the menu that she even wanted to order. She asked the waiter a lot of questions. Then she noticed her mom and great-aunt frowning at her.

"What?" Lily said, annoyed.

Her mom winced. "Keep your voice down. You're nearly yelling."

"Oh, sorry." Lily took out her ear-buds.

"And please don't listen to your music here," her mom whispered. "You're here to connect with your great-aunt and this celebration, not live in a bubble."

What is context?

Comic Sense compared context to an ocean. Context is everything you are in—the place, time, situation, and people nearby. An action is okay or not okay depending how well it fits with the context.

Context is also like a jigsaw puzzle. Pieces of the puzzle are already in place, linked together to create a big picture. When you do or say something, you're adding a new piece into the puzzle. It has to connect with what's already there.

Context is like a JIGSAW PUZZLE.

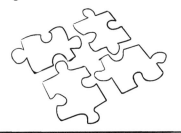

Your words and actions have to fit with what's going on around you, like puzzle pieces linking to what's around them.

The shapes and colors have to match.

Everything has to connect to fit the "big picture."

Just throwing pieces down or trying to jam them in where they don't fit won't work.

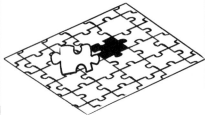

The right pieces slip effortlessly into place.

1. The context puzzle

You can think of context as a set of invisible tabs from you to everything around you. Just like in a puzzle, each thing you do has to fit with everything else.

Fitting actions into the context puzzle

Whenever you do or say something, it has to connect. You have to connect your new piece to the other pieces in place. So look around before you yell. What are you trying to attach your yelling to?

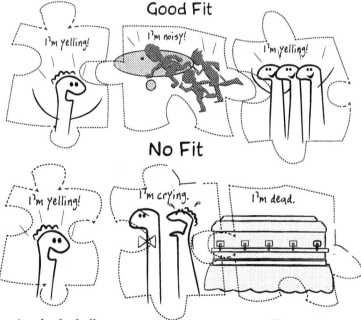

At a basketball game, you can connect your yelling to the noise and yelling in the gym. But at a funeral, there's nothing for your yelling to connect to.

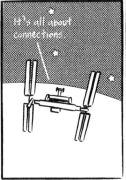

What Connects in the Context?

Context: At a baseball game

- ✔ Cheering and yelling.

- ___ Being quiet and minding your own business.

- ✔ Chatting happily to the people beside you.

- ___ Explaining today's weather systems.

. . . .

Context: In an elevator

- ___ Cheering and yelling.

- ___ Being quiet and minding your own business.

- ___ Chatting happily to the people beside you.

- ___ Explaining today's weather systems.

The first thing that pops into your head

Doing the first thing that pops into your head is like pulling a puzzle piece at random out of the pile and tossing it at the hole. It's not likely to fit, not likely even to land near the right place.

People assume

... that you're aware of the context.

Because they're always aware of it.

People expect

... that you'll match your actions to the context.

If you don't, they assume you're doing it on purpose.

The first thing that pops into your head isn't a thought. It's an impulse. It's just random. You're not thinking about the big picture or looking at the shape and fit.

Impulsive actions comes from thinking inside your head, instead of thinking about everything around you.

Impulsive thinking can be hard to control. But you can learn to fit your actions to the context.

Tips for controlling the first thing that pops into your head:

- **Do a 10-second room zoom:** Before entering a new situation, scan the room for 10 seconds. Look at what people are doing and how the place is set up. Listen to the amount of noise. Figure out the main purpose of the event. Then enter. You'll have enough context information in your head to make good decisions.

- **Connect every action to something:** If you want to be funny, figure out how your joke fits with what people are doing and saying. If you want to talk about something, figure out who is likely to be interested, and when.

What to do

1. **Zoom the room.**
   Be aware what's there and what's going on.

2. **Connect your actions to something or someone.**
   You only have to fit one thing to fit into the context puzzle.

Jed was overwhelmed when he

arrived at the party. So instead of just jumping in, he took the time to scan the room. He wanted to fit in.

There were people everywhere, and they all seemed to be doing different things. Some were dancing, some were clowning around, some were just talking, some were eating. How could he fit himself to all that?

Then he noticed three friends over by the food table. An impulse came over him to yell, run over, grab some food, and start telling them all the things he was thinking about.

Fortunately, he stopped himself in time. That would have

been a disaster. He would have called attention to himself by being too loud, too quick, and too self-absorbed for the context.

Jed spent another minute scanning the room, taking in the noise level and the amount of activity. Then he walked toward his friends, politely excusing himself and smiling as he weaved around people. He kept his movements slow, and he forced himself to be aware of things going on around him.

When he arrived, his friends looked up and welcomed him with a friendly pat on the back.

2. The people context

People are a big part of the context puzzle. What you do and say links to them. Everyone has links to each other.

You can predict

1 **Connect your actions to the people around you.**
They'll become angry if you don't.

2 **Consider their roles, jobs, and relationships.**
If you fit yourself into the patterns, you'll do the right thing.

To fit into the people puzzle, consider the roles, jobs, and relationships you have with the people around you. Connect what you do and say to fit. If you don't, people can sometimes react very strongly.

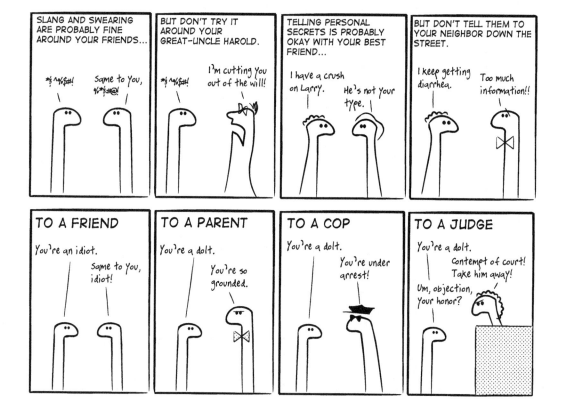

People expect

... that you'll match your actions to everyone's expectations.

Otherwise you'll anger someone.

The web of expectations

People expect you to adapt your words and actions to them. Each person expects things from every other person. Like invisible tabs on puzzle pieces, their expectations have to connect with your actions.

   Everyone's expectations combine together to form a web of expectations. Your job is to be aware what others expect of you, and to do as much as you can to fill those expectations.

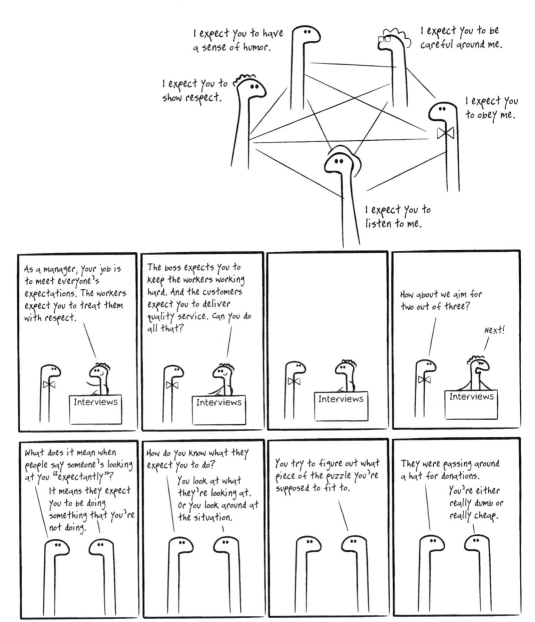

What do people expect?

- **Safety:** They expect you to consider their safety, not just your own. *Example: A mother with a young child expects you not to goof around dangerously near her toddler.*

- **Privacy:** They expect you not to expose their secrets or do anything to embarrass them. *Example: A person with a speech impediment expects you not to comment on his stutter.*

- **Fit:** They expect you to do and say things that connect to the purpose of the group or event. *Example: People sitting in the movie theater near you expect you to sit quietly during the film.*

- **Personal expectations:** Each person expects things based on his/her relationship with you. *Example: Your friend expects you to remember that it's his birthday today.*

What Might They Conclude?

Your boss expects you to be on time and put in a full day's work. Your co-workers expect you to be helpful and cooperative. What might they conclude if you spend an hour of worktime on a video game?

_____ The boss might conclude that you don't really care if you keep your job or not.

_____ Your boss might conclude that you had a hard day and need a break.

_____ Your co-workers might conclude that you expect them to do all your work.

_____ Your co-workers might conclude that you're a fun person.

People assume

... that you're aware what's appropriate for the context.

They believe you know what they know.

The web of assumptions

Asumptions also form a web. People assume you're aware what's appropriate for the context. But every person has their own personal assumptions on top of that.

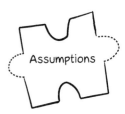

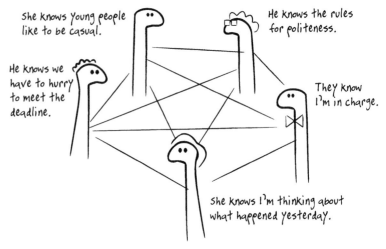

She knows young people like to be casual.

He knows the rules for politeness.

He knows we have to hurry to meet the deadline.

They know I'm in charge.

She knows I'm thinking about what happened yesterday.

What might they make assumptions about?

- **Knowledge:** They assume you know what they know. *Example: Tom just spent 20 minutes explaining the new schedule to you, so he assumes you know about it. But you might have been daydreaming instead of listening.*

She knows about the plan because I just told her.

Dum—de—dum... Daydreaming...

- **Customs and manners:** They assume you have the same customs and manners that they have. *Example: An elderly aunt assumes you will show traditional respect for older people when you're around her.*

- **Priorities:** They assume you have the same priorities they have. *Example: Aid workers in an emergency assume you put the medical needs of the injured ahead of your own selfish needs.*

Hey, could you move that thing out of the way? I need to get to my yoga class.

AMBULANCE

What Might They Conclude?

Your boyfriend assumes you remember he plays hockey every Thursday night. What might he conclude if you buy two tickets to a play for Thursday evening? He might conclude...

____ ...that you really don't want him to go with you.

____ ...that you're angry with him.

____ ...that you meant to buy tickets for a different night.

____ ...that it's a funny joke.

How to handle expectations and assumptions:

- **Think ahead:** If you know people are likely to have expectations or make assumptions, then plan for it. *Example: You have an odd habit that comes up every now and then. It makes people assume you're rude. So talk to them in advance so that you control their assumptions.*

- **Observe:** People communicate their expectations. If you do something wrong, there'll be a signal—a gesture, a facial expression, or a whispered comment. Watch for it. Then quickly offer an explanation.

Predicting a good connection

When your action connects to everything in the context, it's not an accident—it's good planning. You've listened and observed and figured out what will link in with everything around you.

With a bit of thinking ahead, you can predict people's reactions to the things you do :

- ■ **What is everyone doing?** Your actions have to connect to their actions, as well as their mood, energy level, noise level, and thoughts.

- ■ **What do they expect?** You can't know for certain, but look for signals. What are they looking at? How have they reacted to the actions of others? What have they said about what they think will happen next? Adapt your actions to fit their expectations.

- ■ **What do they assume you know?** They assume you know whatever they've told you, either through words or body language. Listening and paying attention will help you figure out their assumptions.

You can predict

1 **Consider what everyone is doing.**
Your actions should fit with theirs.

2 **Consider what they likely expect or assume.**
Otherwise you might lead them to make strange conclusions about you.

3 **Consider their priorities.**
They'll get angry if you put unimportant things first.

4 **Watch their reactions.**
People give strong clues that you're doing the wrong thing.

■ **What are their priorities?** Consider what's important to others. Are they trying to meet a deadline? Get their work done? Relax in peace and quiet? If someone reacts with annoyed body language to your actions, then you've miscalculated what's important to them.

■ **How are they reacting?** People react to the things you do based on the context, their expectations, and assumptions. If they're reacting angrily, you got something wrong. Your actions didn't connect with theirs. Watch and listen to figure out where you're going wrong.

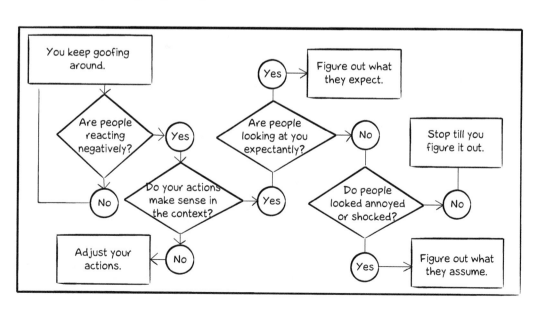

What Connects to the Context?

Context: You're at a tree-planting ceremony in memory of a beloved mayor who died last year.

____ Chat cheerfully with the people around you.

✔ Stand silently, listening and watching for cues about what to do.

....

Context: You're at a bus stop with two people you've never met.

____ Explain to them the intricacies of the bus schedule.

____ Smile politely, but wait quietly for the bus.

....

Context: You're at a school dance.

____ Dance, goof around, and do what your friends do.

____ Bring a book to read.

____ Sit down with someone and tell him/her all about your coin collection.

Summary

Context is like a jigsaw puzzle all around you. Your actions have to connect to that context the way that one puzzle piece fits into the rest of the puzzle.

Common sense means being aware of the context. It means looking for ways to fit your actions

■ **to the place, time, and situation:** Consider

how much your actions make sense given everything that's happening, that's just happened, or that's about to happen.

- **to the people around you:** Reflect on the roles and relationships of the people you're with so that you don't anger or offend anyone.

- **to their assumptions and expectations:** Think about what others want from you. Consider as well what they assume you know.

Beware of doing the first thing that pops into your head. Fitting into the context means taking a few seconds to think before jumping in.

CHAPTER 2
More Personal Perspective

"What's your problem?!" Sam yelled.

Mia was taken aback.

"Hey, all I said was you need a haircut," she said.

"Whose business is it of yours?" Sam countered angrily.

Whoa, what was happening here? Was this Sam, her usually calm-and-quiet boyfriend? "Why are you so bent out of shape about a haircut?"

Sam grimaced. "I don't need my girlfriend telling me what to do with my hair."

"O-kay. So-rry."

"And you don't have to say it so sarcastically." Sam frowned and went quiet for a moment. "My parents have been on my case about my hair for weeks. I guess it's getting on my nerves. Sorry about getting so angry."

What is personal perspective?

Comic Sense described personal perspective as a camera lens on everyone's shoulder. This camera lens affects how they see the world. People look at the world through their own point of view. They don't look at the world through yours.

Personal perspective is also like colored glasses. These glasses darken, lighten, filter, tint, and distort what someone sees. Their likes, dislikes, personalities, emotions, priorities, and memories get in the way of seeing things as they really are.

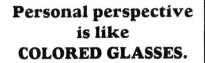

Personal perspective is like COLORED GLASSES.

One person's glasses might be colored by dreams and ambitions. Others might be colored by fears.

I'm going to be a movie star!

I'm going to be a failure.

What people see has a lot to do with what's in their thoughts and feelings.

I feel down today. Wow, this tie looks stupid!

Their thoughts and feelings highlight certain things and hide others.

I see red, red roses.

I see thorns.

No two people have the same colored glasses.

Man, it's dark in here!

Man, it's bright in here!

Personal perspective filters what people see.

1. Personality

Personal perspective has a lot to do with personality. Everyone's personality is different, and it affects how each person sees the world.

Your personal perspective and your personality both come from what's inside you. They create a pair of colored glasses that you see the world through.

Some of the things in your glasses come from your genes, and some of it comes from your life experiences.

Genetics   Life Experiences   Personal Perspective
and Personality

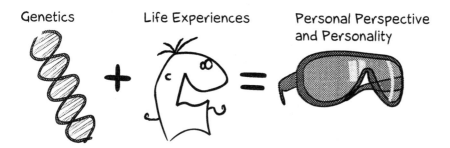

You're born with certain parts of your personality, and you learn the rest. The combination creates your personality and affects how you see the world.

Personality traits

There are lots of personality quizzes on the internet that'll tell you about personality traits.

These tests aren't magic ~ you input information about what you like and dislike, and the tests eventually tell you what you like and dislike. But they're fun to do and can help you understand different personalities.

Here are some of the popular personality traits mentioned in personality quizzes:

Introversion and extroversion

- **Introverts**. Introverts are quieter people. They get their energy from the things going on inside their heads, such as their thoughts, books they're reading, their hobbies, and learning. They tend to have a small number of very close friends. Sometimes they need to be alone.

- **Extroverts**. Extroverts are outgoing and social people. They get their energy from people and action, such as team sports, parties, and shows. They tend to have a large number of acquaintances but few close friends. If things are too quiet, extroverts start to crave action and conversation.

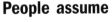

People assume

... that their personality is the normal personality.

It takes a long time to learn that there's no such thing as a normal personality.

"Every time I go to a party, I see

the same thing," Ron said. "The cool people are all in the middle of the room, laughing and talking and dancing. And the uncool people are in pairs around the outside of the room."

"That's because the cool people are extroverts," Mia said. "They like being with lots of people, and they like energy and excitement."

"I guess that's what makes them cool. They get energy from each other."

"And the uncool people are usually introverts," Mia continued. "They prefer to talk to one or two people and really get to know them instead of being with the big crowd."

"So introverts and extroverts don't usually mix together," Ron observed.

"Not when there are lots of people around. Extroverts prefer the energy they get from other extroverts, and introverts prefer the depth and intimacy they get from other introverts."

"So coolness is really just a personality type."

"That's it." Mia grinned. "And just who decided that they're the ones that are cool?"

You can predict

1 **Be aware if someone is an introvert or extrovert.**
Extroverts seek crowds and excitement, and introverts seek quiet and intimacy.

2 **Be aware if someone is open to or wary of adventure.**
Open people choose riskier activities, and wary people choose safer activities.

Attitudes toward risk and adventure

■ **Open to adventure.** These people like new experiences and adventures. They can be very creative and imaginative, but many waste their love of new things on trivial changes or dangerous risk-taking. They can also be fickle, excitable, and quick-tempered.

■ **Wary of adventure.** Some people are afraid of getting hurt. They tend not to be open to new experiences and adventures. They can be shy and unsure of themselves. Some spend a great deal of time worrying.

That looks like fun. It might be risky, but who cares about that?

That looks risky. It might be fun, but who cares about that?

"How is your new business going?"
Lyn asked.

Jack sighed. "We're experiencing a few bumps. My partner Ian wanted to just jump in right away, spend some money, and get going. I wanted to take it more slowly, do more research, and spend cautiously. So it's a bit of a struggle."

"It sounds like a basic personality difference," Lyn said.

"In what way?"

"Your personality is to be cautious. You don't like to take big risks until you're sure what you're doing. But Ian is naturally open to adventure. He'll take more risks than you and deal with the consequences along the way."

"Which way is better for our business?"

Lyn thought for a moment. "Probably both. A business needs someone who's willing to take some risks, but it also needs someone to be the voice of caution."

"So we have both," Ian said. "I guess in a way it's good."

"Once you figure out how to work together, you'll learn to listen to each other. Then you'll get the best of both talents, and your business should do well."

Other personality traits

- **Agreeableness** means getting along with others, fitting in, and making other people feel good. People with high agreeableness are naturally easy to get along with. People with low agreeableness are naturally suspicious and irritable.

- **Conscientiousness** means having self-discipline and doing what you're supposed to do. It's also how much you care about whether you get things done. People have different amounts of conscientousness. People at the low end are more spontaneous but less reliable than people at the high end.

- **Emotional sensitivity** means how much you feel your emotions. Some people feel their emotions very strongly, while other people feel them more mildly. People who feel anger, worry, and sadness very strongly will react more to bad situations than others. They often obsess about situations. In contrast, people with low emotional sensitivity don't get bothered by situations.

You can predict

1 **Be aware how agreeable someone is.**
This helps you predict who will be easy to get along with and who will be easily irritated.

2 **Be aware how conscientious someone is.**
This helps you predict how much you can depend on someone to get things done.

3 **Be aware how emotionally sensitive someone is.**
The more sensitive, the more likely they are to over-react.

What Personality Trait Does This Show?	
Trait	**Action**
High conscientiousness	Sue always gets her chores done before she watches TV.
Low conscientiousness	Lou does his homework on the bus on the way to school. Sometimes he doesn't finish, but he doesn't care too much.
_____ _____	Tony likes wilderness camping.
_____ _____	Tim likes holidays in five-star hotels with a good reputation.
_____	Mike finds social chit-chat and wild parties tiring.
_____	Mary craves conversation and fun after she's been quietly studying for hours.
_____	Lisa gets upset about things that don't seem to bother anybody else.

Living with personalities

There's not much point in hoping that someone will change his/her personality. It's not likely to happen. Most personality traits stay more or less the same forever.

You're better off learning how to accept and adapt to other people's personalities.

Tips for getting along with personalities:

- **Learn and observe.** Take the time to listen to your friends. You need to understand how their personality works and how they see the world.

- **Enjoy differences.** Try not to think of personality differences as something bad. Personalities are interesting. When you learn to see the world the way someone else sees it, you become wiser and more perceptive.

- **Avoid demanding perfection.** There's no such thing as a perfect personality or a perfect way to see the world. It can be frustrating when people don't see things the way you do, but be aware that it's just as frustrating for them.

- **Don't expect other people to think and feel the way you do.** People are very different. If you assume they see the world the same way you see it, then you'll have expectations that get in the way of working together.

- **Don't assume people are arguing with you.** Sometimes when people say things that disagree with what you've said, they're simply trying to show you that other people see things differently. This is not the same as arguing. The person isn't trying to make you change your perspective—he/she just wants you to accept other perspectives.

People expect

... that you'll make an effort to get along with others. *And that you'll be curious enough to learn about other people's personality quirks.*

- **Recognize resentment.** When people resent you, because of things you say or do, they can start avoiding you or ignoring you. You might mistakenly decide that this person has a quiet or antisocial personality. But really, this person is angry with you.

Before deciding that someone's personality is the cause, ask.

- **Recognize unhealthy personalities.** Some people have personality problems. They can be delusional, depressed, anxious, obsessive-compulsive, or aggressive. You still have to learn to get along with these people, but don't feel bad if you can't get the relationship to work perfectly.

"I just got a new job. What should

I do on the first day? Get started working hard? Spend time listening to the boss?"

Jill looked questioningly at Lily.

"You can do those things," Lily said, "but you might want to spend most of your time learning about your co-workers' personalities."

Jill was suprised. "Why? That seems like a total waste of time!"

"Because you have to work with them. You probably hope everyone works the same way you do, but that's not realistic. Everyone has a different personality, and everyone has their own way of working with others."

"I don't get it. Can you give me an example?"

"Well, when you're working on a team, you need to know which people are conscientious. They'll be good organizers. You'll need to know who's open to adventures. They'll come up with new ideas and have energy for new programs. And watch for sensitive people who take criticism personally. You'll need to choose your words carefully to avoid hurting their feelings."

2. Your own personality

In *Comic Sense*, you learned that people see themselves in a personal mirror. This mirror is distorted because you see yourself from inside your head, not from outside (like everyone else).

Your personality is part of your mirror. You probably aren't aware of your personality because it feels normal to you. But that's part of the distortion. Nobody's personality is normal.

If you've ever watched a video of yourself or listened to a recording of your voice, you were probably startled by how different you look and sound. Seeing yourself as others see you can be a shock.

Remember that from inside your head, you look at yourself through your feelings, wants, desires, and your need to feel good about yourself.

Other people see you through what you say, what you do, and what you look like.

People assume

... that you know who you are.
They believe you see yourself the way they see you.

People expect

... that you will try to control your personality quirks.
They expect you to be aware of who you really are.

I'm clever, I'm kind, and I'm strong. Kind of. Sort of. At least, that's how I'd like to see myself.

I've decided I'm a people person.

I serve humanity best when I am using my charm, communication skills, and warm heart to make people's lives more joyful.

So are you going to get a job in a nursing home? Or maybe in a help center?

Are you kidding? Who wants to work with people like that?

You can prioritize

1 Become realistic about your
own personality
...before...

2 Figuring out what to do
about someone else's
personality.

Managing your own personality:

■ **Get second opinions.** When you need to make important decisions, ask other people for their opinions. They see the situation differently from you, so they'll give you information that you don't have.

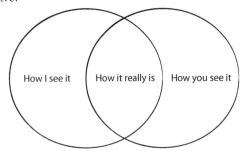

How I see it | How it really is | How you see it

Well, doc, I diagnosed myself using the internet. But I thought maybe I should come in for a second opinion.

■ **Explain in words.** Don't assume people know what you think. They know only what they think—unless you explain how you see things differently.

■ **Respect and be respected.** If you show respect for the personality quirks of other people, they're more likely to respect and accept yours. Life is easier if people accept your personality, so work on making yourself easy to live with.

Managing Your Personality: True or False?

_____ You believe your driving skills are good enough to take your driver's test. But you should get other opinions first.

_____ You're late, but you can just assume that everyone there knows how hard mornings are for you.

_____ Your best friend is often disorganized. You should not have to put up with that.

_____ You have the right to tell people what they should be doing.

3. Saving face

Saving face means saving yourself from embarrassment. People want to feel good about themselves, so they don't like to feel embarrassed. They do and say things to protect how they look to other people.

Saving face is part of someone's personal perspective. You can think of it as a mask of anger or blame that people wear when they want to hide their real feelings.

People can behave in very illogical and unreasonable ways when they're trying to save face. To them, what's important is protecting themselves from embarrassment, not being right or sensible.

Saving face is important to

- **powerful, influential people:** They always want to appear calm and in control.

"Where's the dough from the bank

robberies we did last month?" someone asked.

Lee felt a harsh wave of fear and anger. He'd been the gang leader now for over a year, and the last thing he was going to do was admit that he'd lost that money on a bet.

Instead, he frowned, swore, and looked around the group.

"Somebody took it!" he snarled. "Which one of you was it?!"

The other gang members looked surprised. Some frowned and looked at others.

"It was the new guy!" Lee suddenly pronounced. "Let's get him!"

You can predict

1 **Powerful and important people need to save face.**
They will lie or deflect blame to keep their image.

2 **Sensitive people need to save face.**
They will deflect blame to avoid strong feelings.

■ **sensitive or self-conscious people:** They get hurt easily.

Sheila listened while the examiner

explained the mistakes she'd made in her driving test.

She felt ready to cry.

To cover up, she gave a nervous laugh and tried to make a few jokes.

The examiner was not amused and failed her.

How to tell if someone is saving face

■ **They act illogically.** They say things that are obviously false. They know you know they're lying, but they hope you'll pretend along with them.

■ **They look emotional.** People saving face feel desperation. They usually look angry or fearful (or both at the same time). Sometimes they have a fake, too-big smile that doesn't crinkle their eyes.

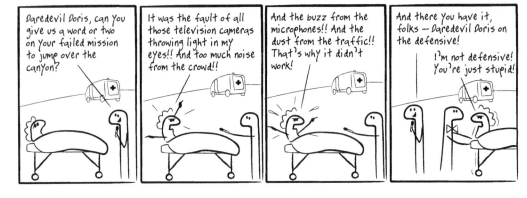

- **Their voice is too strong.** If they're angry or fearful, their voice will be loud or high-pitched. If they're pretending to be happy, they'll sound overly happy.

Who is Trying to Save Face?

The boss discovers that the group report is done not on time. She demands to know why not.

_____ Sue accuses Tim of not doing his share of the work, even though she took the most time off.

_____ Tim feels embarrassed by Sue's accusations and tries to change the subject.

_____ Bert writes everything that happened on paper to give to the boss later.

_____ Tina admits that it was partly her fault because she was late compiling the statistics.

Defensiveness

Defensiveness is a kind of face-saving. People often become defensive when they feel they're being criticized.

Most people like to feel good about themselves, so they feel attacked when someone criticizes them. Suddenly, someone wants them to feel bad about themselves. They feel cornered, insulted, and bewildered.

And then they get angry. They over-react, often yelling, blaming the person who's criticized them, or storming out of the room. Or they sit silent and angry, with their arms folded tight.

Defensiveness is their way to try to save face. But in many ways, by over-reacting, they embarrass themselves further.

Her complaints make me feel bad about myself. I hate that feeling. I want to push that feeling away.

People assume

... that criticism is an attack of them personally.

They don't want to confront their failings.

People expect

... that you will avoid making them feel defensive.

They want you to talk in a way that allows them to save face.

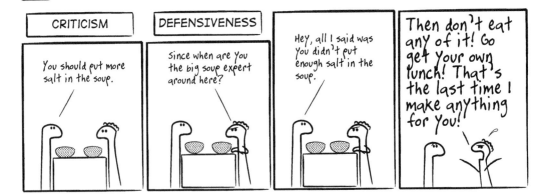

Body language and defensiveness

When people feel defensive, they use defensive body language. Here are some typical gestures, expressions, and actions of defensive people:

- Arms folded across the chest.

- Hands covering ears.

- Eyes shut tight or head turned away.

- Hand held out to say "stop" ~like a shield pushing the other person away.

- Aggressive questions and accusations.

Who's Being Defensive?

The boss discovers that the group's report is done not on time. She starts lecturing them about their responsibilities and asking questions.

_____ Sue folds her arms across her chest and mumbles to Tim that the boss is usually late too.

_____ Tim feels embarrassed but listens and then admits that he hadn't been reading all his emails.

_____ Bert gets angry and starts asking questions back, especially about how much preparation time the team had been given.

_____ Tina accuses the boss of being unfair.

How to avoid making people defensive

People need to save face. When you criticize or complain, they become defensive. Even if you complain about an object, if they own that object, they might feel offended.

Here are some suggestions for complaining without making someone defensive.

- **Use neutral language.** Avoid hurtful, angry, or opinionated words. Use words that aren't hurtful yet also aren't complimentary.

- **Use softening phrases.** You can reduce the impact of a complaint by adding softening phrases to the beginning, such as *I believe*, *I think*, *Perhaps*, etc. Softer phrasing lets the person take responsibility for the problem without taking blame.

- **Phrase criticism as a question.** Soften a complaint is by asking it instead of telling it. *I found this computer doesn't work right. Do you think it might be broken?*

- **Include an apology.** Don't apologize for the problem if it's not your fault. But you can apologize for something else. Any apology-sounding phrase helps your complaint feel less like an attack.

What to do

1 **Zoom the room.**
   Be aware what's there and what's going on.

2 **Fit your actions to something or someone.**
   You only have to connect to one thing in the context puzzle.

What to do

1 **Choose words carefully.**
   Neutral language and softening phrases reduce defensive reactions.

2 **Phrase criticism as questions.**
   This helps deflect the blame.

3 **Include an apology.**
   The other person knows it's not your fault, so you're just doing it to be kind.

- **Use "you" carefully.** Using the word *you* makes a complaint sound more like an attack. Instead of saying *You need to honor the warranty*, say *The store should honor the warranty*. You can even use *we*: *Is there something else we can try?*

Email: First version

You sold me a Model DX4 converter, and it's already not working. What a piece of junk!

I demand a full refund immediately.

Email: Revised version

Last week, I bought a Model DX4 converter from your website. Today, it's already stopped working.

Perhaps it has a manufacturer's defect. But I'm sure you would like to protect your business' reputation and retain me as a long-time customer.

I would like to request a full refund and return the converter.

What to do

1 **Avoid using *you*.**
Use we *or* I *statements to avoid making accusations.*

2 **Make it easy for the person to shift blame.**
This allows them to save face while still accepting your complaint.

3 **Avoid embarrassing the person**
Never criticize or complain in front of others.

4 **Never say *I told you so*.**
You want to avoid suggesting that the person is stupid.

- **Provide opportunities to shift the blame.** People feel better about solving complaint problems if they can feel as if someone else is being blamed. You can shift the blame to someone else: *I think there might be a manufacturer's defect in this computer. I haven't been able to get it to work right.*

- **Avoid having an audience.** If there are people behind you, speak softly. Loud complaints are embarrassing. If possible, ask to speak to the person in private.

- **Avoid saying "I told you so."** Embarrassing and criticizing damages relationships. Saying *I told you so* (even if you did tell them so) tells someone that he/she is stupid. Instead of saying *I told you so*, focus on helping the person solve the problem.

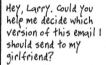

Hi Louise. You gave me a key that doesn't work. It's crap. You managed to get the lock broken. I told you it wouldn't work! So are you going to tell me how to use this key or what?

Hi Louise. Remember that key you gave me? I think there's a problem with it. It didn't work, and the lock's broken now. Any ideas on how we can make it work?

Which Complaints Will Make People Defensive?

_____ You wrecked it.

_____ I'm sorry, but I can't accept a substitution for the one I ordered.

_____ I don't care if other customers are listening! I demand satisfaction now!

_____ Maybe it's a problem from the regional office. But I'm hoping we can solve it here.

_____ I told you you needed to buy more insurance!

_____ I'd like to discuss the problems with this program. Can we go somewhere private?

_____ This is a crappy product, and you're a crappy sales clerk.

How to avoid becoming defensive

It's not fun receiving a complaint or confessing a big mistake. But if you want to keep your relationships and your job, you have to learn to avoid becoming defensive.

At work:

- **Remember your job.** You're not being paid to take care of your feelings, but to take care of customers. Avoid taking customer complaints personally. They're really complaints about your employer, not you. Your job is to calmly fix the problem.

- **Use results words.** When people complain, they want you to talk about results. They don't want to hear more about problems. So talk about positive things. Focus on what you *can* do, not what you *can't* do.

INSTEAD OF	SAY
It's impossible to repair your computer today.	We can have your computer ready by this time tomorrow.

- **Avoid making excuses.** Your employer wants you to solve problems, not save face. So when your supervisor tells you what you're doing wrong, say *Thank you, I'll try that*. Avoid making excuses or blaming someone/something else. Your job is to take the blame, fix the problem, and show respect for your boss.

What to do

1 **Be a professional.**
Don't take work-related criticism personally.

2 **Focus on the positive.**
Tell people what you can do, not what you can't do.

3 **Don't make excuses.**
Take responsibility and fix the problem.

4 **Be humble.**
Admit errors and apologize

5 **Take it in good humor.**
People respect you if you stay calm. You don't have to get angry about criticism.

"I hate this job! Everybody just gets me in trouble all day!"

Joel was ready to quit.

"Why do they do that?" Sue asked him.

"By over-reacting to everything I say!" Joel said. "And then complaining to my boss!"

"Then try using different words," Sue said. "Think about what you would want to hear if you were a customer. Instead of saying what you can't do, tell them what you can do. And don't complain back or make excuses."

"It just makes me mad when people complain at me!"

"Then think of it as complaining to your boss, not to you," Sue said. "That way, you can just get your job done."

With friends:

- **Admit your errors.** It's easier in the long run to be honest than to try to avoid blame and embarrassment. People admire honesty.

- **Use humor.** If you feel hot anger bubbling up, make a small joke to give yourself a few seconds to cool off and think. A legitimate complaint or criticism is not a personal attack, and you shouldn't respond as if it is.

Which Would Help Avoid a Defensive Reaction?

_____ When my boss criticizes my work, I think of the complaint as being against the task he's talking about, not against me personally.

_____ When friends criticize me, I listen and apologize.

_____ When my parents complain, I think sarcastic comments in my mind and stomp off to my room.

_____ To avoid making customers angry, I talk politely and focus on solving their problems, not making excuses.

4. The subconscious mind

People see the world through the lens of their *subconscious mind*. The human mind is very complex. The part you think with—the *conscious mind*—you know fairly well.

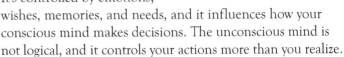

Beneath that is your much more powerful *subconscious mind*, which is full of all the thoughts you're not aware of. It's controlled by emotions, wishes, memories, and needs, and it influences how your conscious mind makes decisions. The unconscious mind is not logical, and it controls your actions more than you realize.

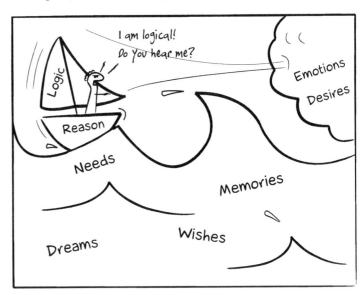

What's in the subconscious mind?

- **Social needs:** for love, belonging, friendship
- **Personal needs:** for dignity or purpose
- **Desires:** for wealth and security, for love and relationships, for escape from sadness, etc.
- **Fears:** of failure, death, truth
- **Anger:** revenge, envy, jealousy
- **Insecurity:** low self-esteem
- **Memories:** childhood memories, yesterday's events, bad and good experiences
- **Wishes:** goals, fantasies, greed

People assume

... that their actions are always based on their decisions.

They aren't aware of the power of their emotions and subconscious wishes.

The subconscious mind is powerful enough to trick your brain into creating "logical" reasons to back up whatever it wants. It helps you create the illusion that you're being sensible.

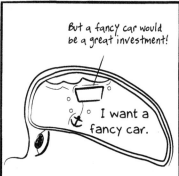

Tina was on a weight-loss diet.

She'd written a list of healthy foods to eat and created meal menus so that she wouldn't go off track.

But suddenly this afternoon, she realized was standing in front of the fridge with the door open. Her hand had already pulled out some treats.

"How did that happen?" she thought in dismay as she shut the fridge door. "I wasn't even thinking. Did I sleepwalk?"

She grabbed herself a healthy snack and headed back to her desk.

But an hour later, she found herself back at the fridge again. Was she losing her mind? What was making her go to the fridge to get forbidden snacks?

That evening, she packed up all the goodies and took them to her brother's house. That way if she did wind up at the fridge again, there'd be nothing to tempt her.

Tricks of the subconscious mind

The subconscious mind is very good at deceiving you and making you or someone else believe things that are illogical or completely false.

Here are four tricks the subconscious mind uses to make you do what it wants you to do.

1. Rewards

People always have a reason for their actions. No matter how illogical the action appears, they are getting some kind of *reward* for doing it.

The reward might not be easy to see, but it's important to be aware that the reward is there.

A reward is either *getting something good* or *avoiding something bad*. If there is no reward, the person will stop doing the action.

The more someone's actions don't make sense, the more you need to consider what rewards they see from their perspective. People's actions make sense if you understand what the rewards are for that person.

You can predict

1 **People do things because of the rewards they get.**
   When there's no reward, they stop doing it.

2 **People are not always aware of the rewards behind their actions.**
   But you can often figure them out by observing the person for a while.

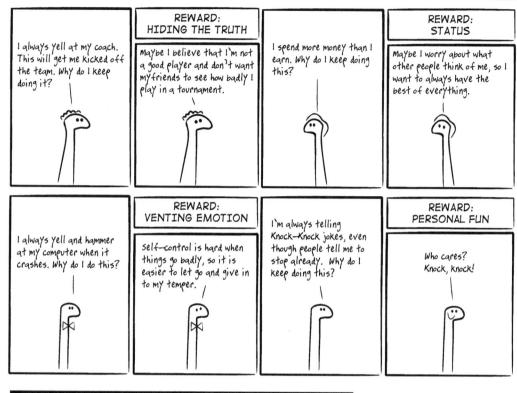

Which Ones are Rewards?

_____ Getting elected

_____ Avoiding saying an apology

_____ Avoiding chores

_____ Feeling excitement and fun

_____ Punishing your worst enemy

_____ Getting lost

Inner rewards and outer rewards

There are two main types of rewards: *inner rewards* and *outer rewards*.

Inner rewards are rewards that are built into the activity. If you like playing tennis, then the feeling of fun is your reward. It's an inner reward because it can't be removed from the activity.

■ **Examples of inner rewards:** enjoyment, interest, sensations, friendship, success, pride

Outer rewards are extras. They're not built into the activity. If you like playing tennis because you get admiration from the spectators, then status is your reward. It's an outer reward because it can be taken away (such as when there are no spectators or when you lose the match).

■ **Examples of outer rewards:** money, status, security, gifts, praise, admiration

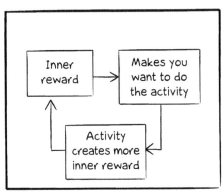

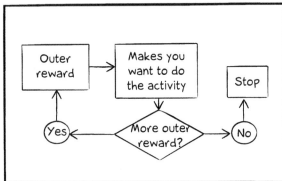

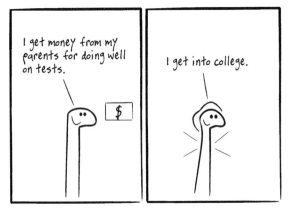

Tony loved playing his drums.

He'd play for hours every day, just to feel the energy and rhythm.

This drove his uncle crazy. He hated the noise.

So the uncle dreamed up a clever way to get Tony to stop playing his drums.

He offered to pay Tony five dollars for every half-hour he played the drums. Tony was only too glad to take the offer.

Why not get paid to do something you love?

So for two weeks, Tony played his drums and got paid. But then his uncle revised his offer. He said it was costing him too much money. He would be able to pay just fifty cents per half hour now.

Tony was incensed. Fifty cents for a half hour of drumming? It was hardly worth it.

So he quit playing drums.

Inner or Outer Reward?

_____	Getting paid money
_____	Feeling wonderful
_____	Knowing you're succesful
_____	Becoming popular with cool people
_____	Feeling proud of yourself
_____	Being admired

2. Rationalizing

Rationalizing means making excuses in your mind for avoiding things you don't want to do or for doing things you know you shouldn't. You can rationalize to avoid responsibility, ignore an unpleasant truth, or justify a bad decision.

Rationalizations feel logical, so you're always tempted to believe them. They help you feel good about yourself while you do something bad.

When you see someone making illogical choices, consider whether he/she is rationalizing to avoid something he/she doesn't like.

People assume

... that their rationalizations are logical.

They don't want to believe that their emotions are in control of their mind.

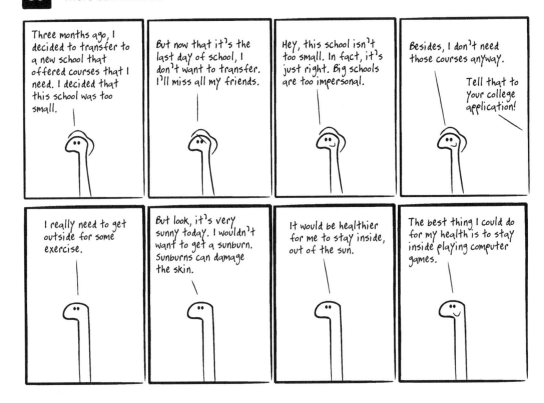

Rationalizing to yourself:

A person illegally evades paying taxes. He rationalizes it to himself by saying that the government just wastes money.

A person buys an expensive new car that she doesn't need. She rationalizes it to her friends by saying the old car wasn't reliable anymore.

A student fails to get into a university. He rationalizes it to his family by saying he didn't really want to go there anyway.

A person is greedy and never gives money to charities. He tells himself that lazy people don't deserve his money.

An athlete in training sneaks food that aren't on her training diet. She tells herself a couple of cookies won't make any difference.

I didn't finish my report on "Rationalizing and Avoiding Responsibilities." I took too many breaks because it was so boring. Can I at least get marks for doing field work?

Find the Rationalizations

_____ "They cheated, so that means I'm allowed to cheat."

_____ "I lost the game fair and square."

_____ "We made illegal changes to these documents because our client pays us to get him as much money as possible."

_____ "It's not my fault I killed someone. I was just following orders."

_____ "I apologize. I shouldn't have done that."

_____ "If you hadn't been so argumentative, I wouldn't have hit you."

_____ "If we don't destroy the environment to get these minerals, then someone else will."

How to avoid rationalizing

- **Listen for ideas that are too good to be true.** Rationalizations make bad things sound acceptable, or even good.

- **Watch for persuasive tricks.** If someone wants you to buy something or do something you don't feel comfortable doing, he/she may use rationalizations to brush away your discomfort. If the person is being too persuasive, then walk away.

Everybody else over-spends. See? There's nothing wrong with it.

Are you sure?

- **Start with evidence and move to the conclusion.** Rationalization starts with a *conclusion* (what you or someone wants to believe) and then creates *evidence* that seems to support it. Whether alone or in a group, you can avoid rationalization by insisting on starting with the evidence.

You can predict

1 **People rationalize to get a reward.**
The reward is often avoiding a negative truth.

2 **Manipulators use persuasive tricks you make rationalize a bad decision.**
If it seems too good to be true, it probably is.

3 **Be logical.**
Always start with the evidence and move toward a conclusion.

People assume

... that they deserve good things.

Everyone else is less deserving.

3. Self-serving Biases

A bias is an assumption you make so that you can feel good about yourself, regardless of the facts. Biases are related to saving face.

The most common self-serving biases are about what you deserve and what other people deserve. You want to feel good about yourself, no matter what, you so refuse to believe that other people are more deserving than you are.

You use these biases to make yourself feel good. When good things happen to you, you'll tend to give yourself all the credit. When bad things happen to you, you'll tend to blame anything or anyone but yourself.

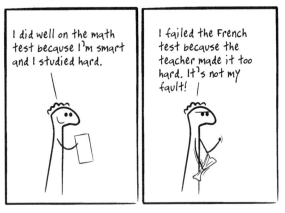

Clever people know they can manipulate you by appealing to your biases.

But when good things happen to someone else, you'll tend to give the credit to anyone or anything except that person. When bad things happen to someone else, you'll tend to blame him/her.

Jon's car got stolen after being left
unlocked in front of his house.

"It's his own fault," Meg's said when she heard the news. "He should have known better. He should lock his car."

"But everybody forgets to lock their car once in a while," Jake countered.

"He's got to learn to remember to lock it every time!" Meg said firmly.

Two weeks later, Meg's car was stolen after being left unlocked in front of her house.

"Well?" Jake said. "Now it's you. What do you think about car theft now?"

"The police aren't doing their job protecting us," she complained. "We aren't safe in our own neighborhoods. That's why my car got stolen!"

You can predict

1 People take credit for good things that happen to them.
They believe they're the good guy.

2 People don't give credit for good things that happen to other people.
They can't believe that someone else is more deserving than they are.

How to deal with self-serving biases

■ **Accept your mistakes, and help others accept their mistakes.** People use biases to avoid feeling blame for not being perfect. But nobody is perfect. If you can help people (including yourself) accept failure, then you allow yourself to learn from your mistakes. If you convince yourself that it wasn't your fault, then you end up living with illusions.

■ **Allow people to save face.** Sometimes people use biases when they're around other people. Avoid bringing attention to the biases, or you'll embarrass and anger the person. Wait till you're in private to question the biased logic.

■ **Be fair:** Whatever you expect for yourself, expect the same for everyone else. If you expect to get credit for your hard work, then give other people credit for theirs. If you allow yourself to make excuses, then accept that other people will make excuses too.

Which Are Examples of Self-Serving Bias?

When there's an accident at work:

_____ If you're in the accident, you'll blame it on the equipment or the other workers.

_____ If you're in the accident, you'll blame it on your poor safety skills.

_____ If someone else is in the accident, you'll blame it on their poor safety skills.

_____ If someone else is in the accident, you'll blame it on the equipment or the other workers.

12302786397809789658

4. Negative mirrors

The subconscious mind can distort how you see yourself. Emotions, wishes, and desires get in the way of thinking clearly.

As a result, you usually aren't a good judge of yourself. Other people have a more accurate picture of who you are.

Some people believe only bad things about themselves. Their mirror is clouded by negative feelings and bad memories. They have low self-esteem and believe everything they do is lousy, even when it's good.

Sometimes the reason is *fear of failure*. They don't believe they can be successful, so they make sure they don't try.

When people have a negative self-view, their actions can appear very irrational. They do things to make their situation worse instead of better.

Jane tells everyone she wants to

go to college. But deep down, she doesn't think she's smart enough, even though her grades are good. She's afraid she might not even get accepted.

So she "accidentally" forgets to mail in the application form in time for the deadline.

Now she can tell everyone that she didn't get in because of the late application, not because she didn't get accepted.

Luke is at college, and he's having

difficulty. Deep down, Luke believes he isn't smart enough for college. So instead of keeping up, he's been letting his work slide.

His instructors call him in for a talk. They tell him he has to complete three short assignments in order to pass his courses. These assignments will only take one day each to complete, and the instructors tell him he can do them easily.

While walking away from the appointment, Luke decides it will be impossible to finish these assignments.

So instead, he quits school.

Now he can tell his friends he had to quit because he was behind in his work, not because he wasn't smart enough for college.

You can predict

1 **People with negative mirrors make bad things happen.**
They sabotage their own efforts.

2 **People with negative mirrors are afraid of success.**
They duck and hide from opportunities to move ahead.

How to prevent negative mirrors:

- **Accept your emotions.** Everybody feels nervous at times. Nervousness is not the same as incompetence. Accept your emotions as emotions so that they don't cloud up your mirror.

- **Be realistic.** People who are perfectionists often have unrealistic ideas about what they should be able to achieve. When they don't achieve them, they become very self-critical. Instead of being unrealistic, keep your goals reasonable and attainable.

Which are Examples of Negative Mirrors?

_____ Tim's friends and colleagues tell him he's an excellent chef. But he believes his cooking is just mediocre.

_____ Lou has failed three times to get into music theater school. He asks his drama instructor for feedback, and she suggests he lacks the creative energy the school is looking for. He decides not to apply again.

_____ Lia believes she has no friends because she's stupid and ugly. But she has three very close friends who like her very much.

Summary

Personal perspective is like a pair of colored glasses. It affects the way you see the world. Every person has their own unique way of seeing reality.

Working with personal perspective means you have to consider the following:

- **Personalities:** Personalities are partly genetic and partly due to life experiences. People can be introverts or extroverts, low or high in openness to adventure, agreeableness, conscientiousness, and emotional sensitivity.

- **Your own personality:** Be aware of your own personality quirks so you can make yourself likable.

- **Face-saving:** People react to criticism by becoming defensive. You can avoid these reactions by predicting these reactions and taking steps to avoid them.

■ **The subconscious mind:** The subconscious mind is the emotional part of your brain you're not aware of. It can trick you through rewards, rationalizations, self-serving biases, and negative mirrors. You can avoid problems by knowing the signs.

CHAPTER 3
More Relationships

"It's really strange," Dee muttered.
"Lisa and I are good friends. We've been friends for years. But now she doesn't call me anymore."

"Do you feel as if you're friends when you see her?" Jim asked.

"Sort of. She's more cool and distant. But I don't know what changed or why."

"Maybe you got on the wrong path," Jim said. "That can happen. When people are friends, they move together along a path of friendship. Maybe you accidentally took a detour."

"What kind of a detour?"

"Maybe instead of doing things that bring you two together, you've started doing things that pull you apart. Maybe you've been angry too much. Or maybe you've been too controlling. That might make her want to avoid you."

What are relationships?

Comic Sense described relationships as bank accounts. You make deposits of goodwill to your relationship to help it grow. If you withdraw goodwill through acts of neglect, meanness, and disrespect, you end up emptying your account and bankrupting your relationship.

Relationships are also like highways. They have direction and movement. When you're in a relationship, you don't sit still. You keep moving along the route toward a stronger and deeper relationship.

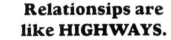

Relationsips are like HIGHWAYS.

You don't sit still in a relationship. Either you're moving forward or it's filling up with weeds.

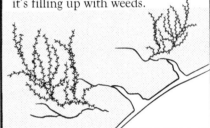

Paying attention to signs and signals will help you get along in the relationship.

STOP WAIT NEVER MIND

Ignoring signs and signals will get you lost. They might even get you or someone else hurt.

STOP *Oops.* **HONK!**

Relationships don't just happen. You have to follow the right route.

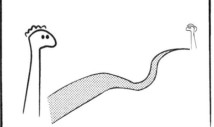

Relationships are a journey.

1. Routes to friendship

The route to friendship is like a highway. If you want to make a friend, you have to put yourself on the route to friendship. It won't just happen on its own.

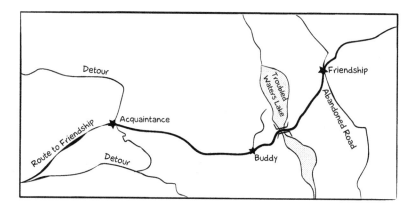

How do you put yourself on the route to friendship? You drive on the same road as that person. You work, talk, listen, share, and have fun together. You keep with it, watching for signs and signals, and avoiding all the detours.

What's on the route to friendship:

- **Listening and learning:** Friendships don't happen until you take the time to learn about your new friend. A person is not a thing, and by listening and learning, you figure out who the person really is.

- **Time:** To become a friend, you need to spend time together. You coordinate your habits and passtimes with the other person. You let things develop without trying to speed.

- **Problems and solutions:** All friendships have problems. These include mistakes, anger, confusion, misunderstandings, and forgetfulness. All these problems can be solved by talking, listening, and apologizing. Problems don't make a friendship weaker: in fact, by working through problems, you strengthen the friendship.

The route to friendship is like a road. You travel together, doing things, sharing things...

...listening to each other, learning, giving in, and taking turns. Just stay on that road and keep going.

I was hoping it was more like a store, where I could just buy a friendship.

Which is why you don't have any friends.

I would try to get it on sale too.

Does the route to friendship include listening, paying attention, and answering when they call?

Yeah! Hey, I think you're finally getting it!

Yep, I got it yesterday.

And it was cheap too.

What was cheap?

This answering machine.

I followed your "route to friendship" advice, and now I have four friends...

But they're all losers.

But you're a loser.

Three friends, then.

Hi, I'm Jake.

Hi, I'm Louise.

BUS STOP

I believe in trying to make one new friend per day. So after I critique the clothes you're wearing, ignore what you're trying to signal to me...

... recite my daily schedule, list my phobias, describe my health issues, pry into yours, and ask you for part of your lunch...

...then maybe we'll be friends!

Or maybe I can start taking a different bus.

Changes along the route

Friendships don't start out as friendships. You may start out as strangers to each other. Even if you take an instant liking to that person, you still aren't friends. You need to travel together for a while before you reach friendship.

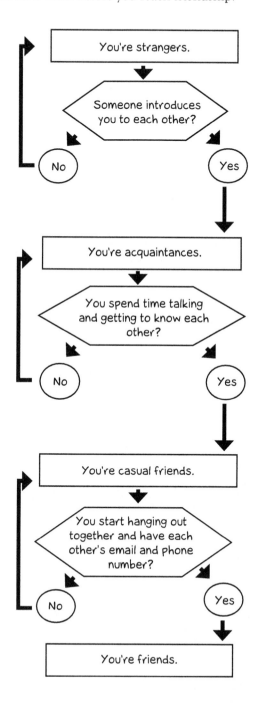

People assume

... that you're aware how close your relationship is with them.

They expect your actions to match your closeness.

You can predict

1 **People like you to respect how close your relationships is.**
Strangers and acquaintances will be alarmed if you act like a friend.

2 **Friendships grow slowly.**
If you rush, people will pull back.

Developing a friendship is a long route. It has a speed limit. If you go past the speed limit—such as trying to push the relationship quickly toward friendship—then you'll annoy and alarm the other person.

Watch for signs that you're going too fast, and slow down.

"Hi, Kate!"Jim waved her over.

"This is my new friend Paul. We met in the elevator a few days ago. Paul, this is my girlfriend Kate."

Jim smiled to himself. He'd done that introduction very nicely. But then he noticed Kate frowning and looking uncomfortable. Paul was backing away.

"Yeah... uh... see ya... I guess," Paul muttered, then walked off.

Jim was bewildered. "What did I say?"

"You called him a friend," Kate answered. "Someone you met in an elevator is just barely an acquaintance. You need to give time to let the relationship develop into a friendship. He was alarmed that you were rushing things."

You're Friends If....

_____ Someone has just introduced you.

_____ You go to the same school and hang out together after class.

_____ You buy coffee at the same coffee shop at the same time every day.

_____ You both belong to a club and often sit with each other.

_____ You were friends in elementary school (even though you never spend any time together now).

_____ You have a friend in common.

2. Exchange relationships

As you move along the route to friendship, *exchanges* become important.

An exchange is any kind of *sharing*. It can be sharing of belongings, food, work, personal information, secrets, or confidences.

Exchanges are important social actions that help cement a growing friendship. They create the intimacy and closeness of a close friendship.

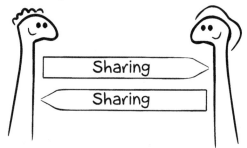

Always remember that strangers don't expect you to share with them. There are no exchange relationships between strangers.

Exchanges as contracts

Exchanges are like *contracts*. When you give something to someone, they become obliged to you. They need to share something back. They may do it right away, or they may do it some other day.

Stay aware of your part in these exchange contracts. You need to return the favor. But avoid using exchanges as a way of forcing a friend to do something for you. People get angry if they feel their friendship is being abused.

People expect

... that you'll avoid **exchanges with strangers.**
Exchanges are part of close relationships.

People expect

... that you'll return their **favors some day.**
But they expect you not to make a big show of it.

Sharing belongings

Sharing your stuff shows that you trust the other person. It communicates that you value your friendship more than your belongings. That friend will lend you something in return, but maybe not right away.

Sharing confidences

Revealing deeply personal information about yourself and listening to your friend's secrets are exchanges. Only close friends share confidences. It shows deep trust.

But sharing confidences is also a contract: by listening, you're bound never to reveal your friend's secrets. If you do, you'll lose everyone's trust and respect.

Sharing food

People share food as they get to know each other. Strangers never share food.

Often food-sharing has special rules. Learn these rules by observing how your friends behave.

- **Sharing treats:** If you have a sharable treat (such as a bag of candy) and your friends around you don't, then you must offer some to each person and say *Would you like one?* They will do the same the next time they have a treat. However, never offer food to strangers.

People expect

... that if you eat in front of them, you'll share.

But this does not apply to strangers.

- **Buying rounds:** Some groups of friends have the tradition of *buying rounds* of food or drink (buying one for everybody). If your friends have this tradition, remember that some day you have to be the one to buy the rounds.

Tips for sharing and exchanges

- **Start with simple exchanges.** For example, offer a new friend a gum, or share your bag of chips. You can also exchange simple factual information about yourself.

People assume
. . . that if you accept someone else buying a round, that you'll buy one too some day.
Friends like being "in debt" to each other a little bit.

- **Don't accept if you don't want to.** A friend has to offer to share treats with you because it's impolite to eat in front of someone. But that doesn't mean you have to accept. Consider whether the person has enough to share. Be kind, not greedy.

- **Keep track.** Remember who has made these exchange gestures to you. If someone has shared food with you, you should return the gesture sometime soon.

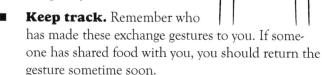

You can prioritize
1 Remembering your debts to others
...comes before...

2 Keeping track of their debts to you.

"Thanks, buddy! I owe you one!"

Jack called as he left the room.

Mark turned to Graham. "What does he mean? Why does he owe me anything?"

"He needed a pen fast, and you lent him yours. So he feels indebted."

"What does he owe me?"

"A more or less equal favor in return," Graham said. "This is what friends do. They do kind things for each other and make a point of paying them back. This keeps all the kindness moving between you. It's like a network of debts that helps to bind the friendship together. You give now, but you don't expect to get repaid until sometime later."

Do You Owe Him/Her One?

_____ He just offered you some chips from his bag. Do you owe him some of your chips (or another snack) some day soon?

_____ She just helped you paint your office. Do you owe her some of your time with one of her household chores some day soon?

_____ He just bought you all a round of drinks at the bar. Do you need to buy a round of drinks for him and the others some day soon?

_____ She just lent you her textbook. Should you look for a way you can repay this favor sometime soon?

_____ He just replied to your email. Do you owe him a reply to his reply?

---

3. Being likable

Making friends requires effort. It doesn't just happen.

Most people try to make themselves likable, and over time, that earns them some friends. They make sure they provide as many benefits as possible to the other person, with very few costs.

What doesn't work

Taking any detour from the route to being liked will make you less likable. Most of these detours have to do with giving in to negative emotions and self-centeredness.

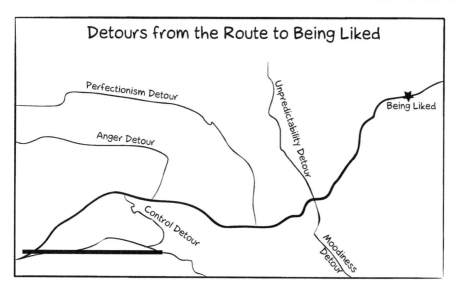

Detours from the Route to Being Liked

1. Controlling others

Controlling means trying to make people do what you want them to do. People dislike it when you try to control them. Ultimatums, manipulations, and demands make you unlikable.

Being a friend is not the same as being an orchestra conductor. Being together doesn't mean you get to tell everyone what to do.

You can prioritize

1 **What the group wants to do**
  ...comes before...

2 **What you want to do.**

How to resist the urge to control others:

■ **Be flexible:** It can be hard to understand that other people have different ideas than you, and that their ideas are just as good (or maybe even better) than yours. You might even resent how much you have to give in to get along with others. But give-and-take is essential for friendship.

■ **Find out what they're flexible about.** Sometimes you can make a deal with friends. You can negotiate parts of your idea and parts of their idea. Find out what they consider important and unimportant and talk about it.

■ **Focus on the relationship, not on the idea.** To be likeable, you have to value people more than ideas. If you have suggested your idea, and your friends don't want to go along with it, then dump the idea and keep the friends. That's better than dumping the friends and keeping the idea.

You can prioritize

1 Focusing on the relationship
   ...comes before...

2 Focusing on your ideas.

2. Anger

People lose patience with you if you're angry a lot. Anger is negative, and it makes you no fun to be with.

You may find that you usually get angry when you aren't able to control another person. You want something, and you can't understand why the other person doesn't do it.

The problem is that you assume that what you think in your head is connected to what someone else does. Your thoughts influence *your own actions*, but they don't influence anybody else's actions.

People who believe there's a connection between their thoughts and someone else's actions get into a spiral of anger.

You can predict

1 **People don't like dealing with your anger.**
   It makes them feel confused and uncomfortable.

2 **Watch for body language of surprise and confusion.**
   It means your anger is driving your friends away.

How to reduce anger:

- Stop and say nothing. In the pause, ask yourself: *What do I want?*

- When you figure out what you want, calmly tell the other person. The other person probably had no idea.

- Once you've explained what you want, you can try negotiating something that works for both of you.

 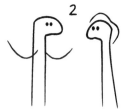 

Jill was furious with her co-worker.

Instead of finishing the report they were both supposed to be working on, Ted was starting work on a new report. Sure, it was more interesting than the one they were supposed to be doing, but the deadline was coming up. That was going to leave Jill with all the work to do.

Jill was angry all day.

Ted came up to her after lunch. "What's up, Jill? You don't look well."

Didn't look well?! Jill lost her cool and started yelling.

"Maybe I'm not well because I have so much work to do! Ever think of that, huh, Ted?!"

Ted stared at her. "Get a grip, Jill. Maybe you need a day off." And he walked away before Jill could say anything more.

Marta came up beside Jill. "Listen, Jill. You're mad about something, but Ted doesn't know what it is. You haven't explained it to him."

"I'm mad because he's leaving me with the whole report to do! And it's his job to do half of it!"

"But just being angry doesn't solve that problem. Your anger doesn't make Ted do anything. There's no connection between your anger and his actions."

Jill frowned in confusion. "What do you mean?"

"Look. Whenever I start feeling angry at someone, I force myself to calm down. Then I think about why I'm angry and what I want or need from the person. Then I go explain that to him or her. If you do that instead of being angry, Ted will know what's going on, and you'll be able to work out a solution."

What to do

1 **Think before you get angry.**
Figure out what you want from the other person.

2 **Calmly explain what you want to the other person.**
This communicates your points, not your emotion.

3 **Negotiate.**
Let the other person make offers.

4 **Find a solution.**
Now you've kept a friend.

3. Moodiness

Like anger, moodiness is a cost to a friendship. Sure, everyone gets down once in a while. But if you're depressing all the time, then you're not fun to be with.

Think of Eeyore in *Winnie the Pooh*. His constant sad mood made it hard for anyone to be his friend.

When you're with others, focus on being positive. If you can't get control of your moodiness and depression, then you should get professional help.

You can prioritize

1 Making other people feel comfortable and respected
...comes before...

2 Being right or correcting errors of fact.

4. Unpredictability

People don't like being around friends who behave bizarrely on purpose. It's okay to be different. But when people are in groups, they have to get along, despite all their differences. To be liked, you have to make an effort to go with the flow.

5. Demanding perfection

People feel put down and embarrassed if someone is correcting them all the time. Pointing out someone's mistakes is considered rude. Nobody's perfect.

If you want to be accepted despite all your faults, then you need to be open and accepting of the faults of others.

"Is it better to be right or to be liked?"

Jana asked.

"Good question," her aunt answered. "But it all depends what you're trying to do."

"What do you mean?"

"If you're writing an exam or making a speech, it's better to be right. But if you're with friends or trying to make new friends, then it's better to be liked. It all depends what you're trying to do."

"I just hate it when facts are wrong," Jana said quietly. "I feel that I have to correct people. I can't leave things wrong."

"You're talking about being fact-right. You also need to think about being people-right. It's a big mistake to harrass people about imperfections when you're trying to be friends."

"So there are different kinds of mistakes," Jana said.

"That's right. Something is correct or incorrect because of your goal. If it takes you in the wrong direction, then it's a mistake."

Find the Likability Mistakes

_____ Jena watches what her friends do and tries to match her actions to theirs.

_____ Lisa does the first thing that comes into her head, even though it doesn't fit with what her friends are doing.

_____ Lou feels grumpy today, and he doesn't feel like trying to be cheerful just because everyone else is.

_____ Ed feels he's right to be angry at his friend, because his friend has made a lot of stupid mistakes lately.

What works

The route to being liked isn't hard, but it means ignoring all the detours and focusing on the road ahead.

Being liked is something you *earn*. It's not something you get just because you were born.

The following tips are the best ways to make yourself likable.

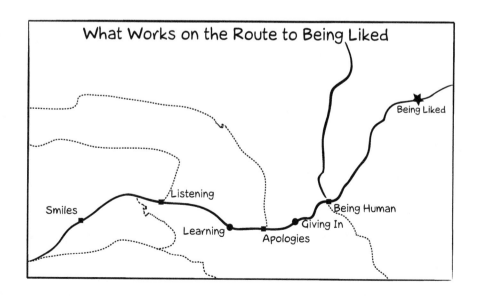

What Works on the Route to Being Liked

1. Smiling a lot

Smiling is an easy way to make yourself likable. A smile communicates not just happiness, but also acceptance, approval, and positiveness. If you want to be liked, it helps a lot to show a lot of acceptance in return.

Smile a lot—with your teachers, the staff at the gym, the store clerk, etc. Smile when you say *please, thank you, you're welcome,* and *excuse me,* when you request something, and when you offer help. Always show good intentions on your face.

I was going to ask Jake to go out with me, but he hasn't smiled at me at all. I think he doesn't like me.

I was going to ask Jake to go bowling, but he doesn't even smile when I talk to him. I think he wouldn't want to come.

I was going to ask Jake to get some fries with me, but I think I'll ask Louise instead. Jake isn't even smiling.

Maybe you should smile more. Oh, like that's going to make a difference to my life!

2. Listening

To be liked, you have to really listen to other people. What are they really saying? What do they really want? It's not enough to be silent, just waiting for your turn to talk again.

When someone's talking to me, I'm always thinking about what I want to say next.

I stop hearing what they're saying. I just watch their mouths flapping.

Meanwhile, I'm rehearsing what I'm going to say and looking for a split second where I can interrupt and jump in. Yeah, but...

Wait! Don't leave! Don't you want to hear what I have to say? What goes around comes around.

3. Learning about people

Likable people are curious about their friends—not in a nosy way, but in a warm and accepting way. Learn whatever you can about your friends. The more you know about them, the more you can do things they like.

4. Apologizing when you make mistakes

Learning to make quick apologies will make you very likable. Everybody makes mistakes. People appreciate when you try to fix your mistakes right away.

"Ken? Could I have a word?"

Dan stood nervously in his co-worker's doorway.

"Sure. Come on in." Ken pulled out a chair.

Dan sank into it. "I want to apologize for my outburst during the meeting. I shouldn't have talked to you that way. I was feeling a bit overwhelmed by all the work, and I let that get to me. Sorry."

Ken nodded. "Okay. Apology accepted."

"So, um, can I get you a coffee or something?"

"Sure." Ken smiled. "Black, no sugar. And thanks for explaining things to me."

People assume

... that you value your friendships enough to fix problems.
Walking away and ignoring problems means you don't care.

What to do

1 **Smile a lot.**
Smiles communicate warmth, openness, and friendship.

2 **Listen a lot.**
People like friends who care enough to learn about them.

3 **Apologize for your mistakes.**
Don't walk away from a problem: fix it.

4 **Adapt to others.**
Sometimes you have to give in.

5 **Be an equal, not a superior.**
People like to feel that their friends are imperfect, just like them.

5. Adapting and giving in

Giving in to what your friends want to do might not feel good. You might want to do things your way. But being a likable person means cooperating, adapting to others, and at least sometimes giving in.

You can't insist on your choices all the time and still be liked. Sure, try to persuade others that your idea is the best. But if they don't agree, then give in with a smile. This shows your friends that you value their friendship more than you value getting your own way.

6. Being human and equal

Don't try to be perfect. Perfection is boring. Besides, people don't like the idea that anybody else is better than they are.

- ■ **Don't try to hide all your faults.** Admitting weaknesses helps bond people together.

- ■ **Avoid bragging.** Nobody likes a know-it-all.

- ■ **Avoid thinking how great you are.** Your thoughts will show. Even if you say something very modest, your face, voice, and body language will give away your thoughts.

"I lost my wallet!" Meg wailed.

Don snorted. "Well, if you wouldn't leave it lying around all the time, that wouldn't happen!"

Meg stiffened as Don left the room. "He's so self-centered," she muttered to Lyn. "All he wants to do is correct people."

Lyn patted her on the arm. "I've lost my wallet a few times too." She grinned. "Just because we lose things, that doesn't mean we're losers, right?"

Meg smiled, and her anger melted away. "You make me feel like an equal, not like an idiot," she said. "That's why I like you."

"Well, try to have some sympathy for Don. He doesn't realize how unlikeable he makes himself!"

Which Ones Are Likeable?

_____ Ruth wanted to insist on everyone doing things her way. But she knew it wasn't fair, so she gave in to the group's plans.

_____ Tim made sure he smiled as he met new people so that they'd consider him approachable.

_____ Lyn knew she'd hurt her friend's feelings, but she resented being pressured into apologizing, so she said nothing.

_____ Fran listened to the discussion, but mentally, she was rehearsing what she was going to say next so that she could interrupt.

_____ Ben is genuinely curious about people and asks lots of questions when he's listening.

_____ When Tim tells her he didn't make the team, Pat tells him she knows why and then lists all his weaknesses as a player.

4. Routes to conversation

So what do you talk about to turn a relationship into a friendship? Your conversation has to match where you are on the route to friendship. Then, over time, you can move it further along the route.

1. Match your conversation to your closeness

Conversation is different depending how well you know the other person. The closer and more familiar you are, the more you can talk about.

Strangers   Acquaintances   Friends   Close friends

With close friends, you can talk deeply about just about anything. With acquaintances or strangers, you have to limit your conversation to safe, neutral topics.

- **Topics for strangers:** greetings, smiles, polite requests and thanks, or comments on the weather. Avoid getting into a deep conversation with a stranger: it weirds them out. Watch for body language that suggests that the person is uncomfortable.

- **Topics for acquaintainces:** events, work, school, jokes, greetings, sports, TV, and pleasantries. You can also talk about things happening around you. Keep it light and happy.

- **Topics for friends:** any topic, provided you've already talked about a similar topic before. Be careful about new topics. Introduce them very gently, observing the other person to make sure they don't look uncomfortable.

People expect

... that you'll adapt your conversation to your closeness.

Otherwise they'll think you're rude (or insane).

1. Match your conversation to the person you're talking to

Think about the person you're talking to. What are his/her interests? What do you know about this person? What's his/her job? His/her relationship or connection to you?

Choose topics that match the people you're with. They're more likely to appreciate the conversation if you match it to their interests, abilities, priorities, and life.

Also consider the person's job or relationship to you. Are there topics you should avoid?

3. Match your conversation to the direction of the conversation

Conversations aren't essays. They don't stick to one topic. They move and change as people make contributions, introduce new ideas, and drop old ideas. Conversations are about relationships, not about topics.

■ **Follow the topic:** Before you start talking, figure out what the topic is. Connect to it. Don't jump in with random, off-topic statements. That communicates that you're self-centered.

■ **No backtracking:** When people drop one conversation topic for a new one, you have to drop it too. Avoid trying to go back and get a dropped topic. Also, don't demand a "replay" if you missed part of the conversation. Keep yourself going in the direction of the conversation.

■ **Don't hog the road:** Conversations are for learning about other people. They're not for making speeches or telling everyone about yourself. People have limited patience for talkers who hog the road.

"Hey! What's happening?"

Paul squeezed his way into the group. But for some reason, the conversation stopped. They were all looking at him.

"Don't mind me," he said quickly.

They gave him one last look and then started talking again. Paul realized he'd arrived right in the middle of a story. That's why they were annoyed. He'd interrupted them.

He listened till they arrived at a topic he found interesting: video games. He had lots to say on that topic and started giving them tons of useful information. When someone tried to change the subject, he reminded the others that they weren't finished talking about video games yet.

Just then, his friend Ted whispered in his ear and pulled him aside.

"You shouldn't hog the conversation like that," he said quietly. "Everyone gets a say, not just you. They want to talk about a variety of topics, not just your favorite topic."

"What should I do then?"

"Spend more time listening and following."

People assume

... that you're watching them for interest and boredom signals while you're talking.

Because they're watching for your signals.

How to tell if someone is interested in your conversation

- **They ignore distractions.** Things might draw their attention for a second or two, but their eyes return to you.

- **They lean forward.** People naturally lean forward when they're listening.

- **They tilt their head.** This means they're considering your ideas.

- **They nod, smile, and make small comments.** They give constant positive feedback while you talk.

- **They gaze at you.** Their eyes are on your face or your hands. When you're talking about a person or object, they're looking at that person or object. They aren't looking around the room.

- **They wait quietly while you speak.** Interrupting is a sign that someone isn't interested in your conversation. Sighing, shifting from one foot to the other, and looking at their hands are all signs that the person isn't listening anymore.

You can predict

1 **People show their interest.**
If you don't see signs of interest, then they're not interested.

2 **People show their boredom.**
They're likely to make an excuse to get away from you.

3 **Boredom annoys people.**
If you bore people often, they won't want to talk to you.

People tell you what they want to talk about.

So what do you think of my new car?

They steer conversations toward or away from topics.

Enough about work. What are you doing this weekend?

How to tell if someone is bored with your conversation

■ **They stop making eye contact.** They look anywhere but at you. This body language reflects their thoughts—they are no longer thinking about you.

■ **They look unhappy.** Their smile seems strained or is fading quickly. Their eyebrows seem to be frowning a little. Their jaw is tight.

■ **They take big breaths, like sighs.** You can actually hear the exhales. Sometimes it seems as if they've taken a breath because they're about to interrupt you. Sighs and exhales are silent signals for you to stop talking.

■ **They look around.** They seem to be looking for an escape. They're distracted by things going on around you. They may even interrupt to point out something interesting. These are strong signals that the person wants you to change the subject.

People expect

... that you'll stop talking when they show signs of boredom.

Because they're trying to let you know they're bored.

Bored or Interested?

_____	Jessie's eyes have started wandering around the room.
_____	Sue leans forward in her chair.
_____	Terry lets out a big sigh.
_____	Tim was looking at your face for a while, but now he's looking at the floor.
_____	Lisa smiles, nods, and makes small comments while you're talking.
_____	Dan tilts his head, as if considering what you're saying.

Summary

A relationship is like a highway. If you follow the route to friendship, you'll end up with a friend.

The route to friendship includes

- **listening and learning:** Only by listening to each other can you learn enough to deepen the friendship.

- **spending time together:** Friendship can't grow if the two people don't spend much time together.

- **facing problems:** All relationships have problems. To stay on the route to friendship, you need to focus on finding solutions to those problems.

Being likable is not an accident. There are things you can do to make yourself likable or not likable. Instead of

- **controlling others**
- **being angry at others**
- **being moody**
- **being unpredictable**, and
- **demanding perfection**

try doing the following:

- **smiling a lot**
- **listening and learning**
- **apologizing for mistakes**
- **giving in some of the time**, and
- **being human and equal.**

Be aware where you are on the route to friendship so that you can make your conversation fit your closeness. The better you know someone, the more you can talk about.

Finally, watch for signs of boredom and interest when you're talking to people. You'll be more likable if you're considerate of others when you're talking.

CHAPTER 4
More Perspective

"Whoa! What are you doing?"

Tim raced over to Rose and pulled the pile of clothes out of her arms, just as she was about to toss them into the fire.

"Stop, Tim!" Rose said, trying to grab the clothes back. "I have to burn them! And you have to wear protective gloves!"

"Why?"

"Because I got head lice. So now I have to burn everything."

Tim snorted and tossed the clothes behind him. "You don't have burn everything! You just have to wash them in hot water and put them in the dryer."

"I don't want to take chances."

"This isn't about taking chances, Rose. It's about over-reacting. Lice isn't a big enough problem to be worth burning all your clothes. You create an even bigger risk with this fire. So help me put it out, please."

What is perspective?

Comic Sense talked about perspective as a lens. A perspective is a way of looking at things. The more different ways you look at a situation, the more perspective you have on what's really going on.

Perspective is also like a ruler. You use perspective to measure something to figure out how big or important it is. You can use several different rules to measure it in several different ways. Once you know how important it is, you'll know how much to react.

1. The perspective ruler

If perspective is a ruler, what does it measure? It measures
bigness and importance. It answers the question *How much?*
The higher the measurement, the more you need to react.

You can think of perspective as a scale from 1 to 5 that
reates how much of a reaction the situation needs.

The Perspective Ruler

Level 5: Emergency.

Level 4: React fast, no time to waste.

Level 3: React.

Level 2: React calmly, no need to hurry.

Level 1: Don't need to react.

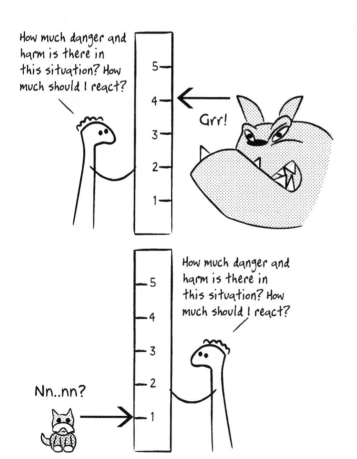

People assume

... that you automatically
measure a situation.

*This is an instinct that has
kept our species surviving for
thousands of years.*

Rate the Importance (1 – 5)

_____ A bomb explodes in the building next to yours.

_____ You fall and scrape your knee.

_____ There's a hole in your wallet, and you've lost all your coins.

_____ A small child has wandered out onto a busy road.

_____ You fall and break your arm.

_____ The conference's microphone system suddenly isn't working.

_____ The key won't work, and you're locked out of the house.

_____ The milk spilled on the floor.

Asking "how much" questions

One way to get perspective is to ask *how much* questions. These *how much* questions help you figure out where they are on the perspective ruler.

Here are some examples of *how much* questions:

- *How much does this matter?*
- *How much time will this take?*
- *How much will he care?*
- *How much will she be inconvenienced?*
- *How much will this matter in the long run?*
- *How much pain will this cause?*
- *How much happiness will this create?*
- *How much should I be concerned?*
- *How much will this cost me (or others)?*
- *How much money will I (or others) make?*
- *How much effort is the right amount?*

What to do

1 **Rate the importance.**
Use a 5-point perspective ruler.

2 **Ask *how much* questions.**
They help you focus on measuring different aspects of the situation.

"My paper is due tomorrow, and I

haven't started it!!" Ana cried. "What do I do?"

"First, let's put it in perspective," Sue said. "How much is the paper worth?"

"Fifteen percent of my grade."

"And how much research do you need to do for it?"

"About one hour."

"And how much time will it take to write?"

"About an hour, once the research is done."

"So it's two hours of work, worth fifteen percent of your grade," Sue said. "That doesn't sound like a crisis to me. It just sounds like one evening of hard work."

Ana groaned. "Off to the library I go."

2. The big deal ruler

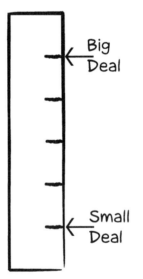

One very important perspective ruler is the *big deal ruler*. It measures whether something is a big deal or not.

A big deal is a situation that really matters. People often say *"Big deal!"* very sarcastically when something is a very small deal and they don't believe they should care about it.

Always measure whether something is a big deal before deciding how to act.

Big deal.

Big hairy deal.

Big super hairy deal.

No deal.

Big deal vs. bigger deal

Often when you're using the big deal ruler, you're comparing one big deal against another. Which is the bigger deal? Which one do you need to focus on? Measure to figure out which one is bigger.

"Help! I have two project deadlines

next week!" Dan said wearily. "Both are important. But which one should I do first?"

"Compare them," Lyn said. "Which one is bigger?"

"The accounting report."

"Which one will make the biggest difference in the long run to the company's profits?"

"The management report."

"Which one does the boss need soonest?"

"The management report."

"It sounds to me as if the management report is more important. So I'd do that one first."

■ **Long-term big deals are a bigger deal than short-term big deals.** Long-term effects last longer, so they're bigger. Just because something is happening now, that doesn't make it the most important. Big deals that are off in the future look smaller than they really are.

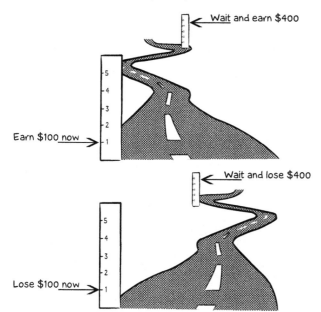

Wait and earn $400

Earn $100 now

Wait and lose $400

Lose $100 now

You can prioritize

1 **Long-term big deals**
  ...are bigger than...

2 **Short-term big deals.**

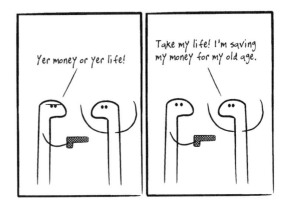

■ **Caring for others is a bigger deal than caring for yourself.** Your relationships are the most important thing you have. As much as possible, put the needs of others ahead of your own needs.

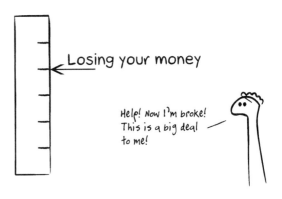

You can prioritize

1 Big deals for other people
...are more important than...

2 Big deals for you.

You can prioritize

1 Big deals about health
...come before...

2 Any other choice.

■ **Health is a bigger deal than preferences.** Going to doctor appointments, eating healthy food, and getting exercise are all more important than doing things that you like. Actions about health are a bigger deal than other choices.

Lisa was ecstatic that she was

accepted to a European university. It had been her goal in life to study abroad.

Once there, she put everything else out of her life and focused on being an excellent student.

However, three months into the program, she wasn't feeling well. Her roommate sent her to see a doctor.

A week later, the doctor called her in for a talk. "The test results show that you have thyroid cancer."

"Yes, I know that," Lisa replied. "I had those tests done before I left home."

"You didn't get the treatment done first?"

"No," Lisa said. "The doctor told me it was slow growing, so I decided not to do it. If I had, I would have had to stay home instead of coming here."

The doctor frowned. "You're lucky we've caught this in time. You start treatment tomorrow. But never put anything in your life ahead of your health!"

What's the Bigger Deal?

_____ You're hungry, and you want to find a place to get some lunch.

_____ Your friend twisted her ankle, and she needs to get to a clinic.

_____ Someone stole $500 from your wallet today.

_____ Your investment company invested your pension money badly, and you won't have enough to live on after you retire.

People expect

... that you'll correct yourself when they tell you you're over- or under-reacting.

They believe you want to have the right perspective.

3. Over-reacting and under-reacting

Things are happening all the time, and one of the jobs of common sense is to help you figure out how much to react. You need to avoid over-reacting to everything...

...and under-reacting to everything.

That's why measuring things accurately is important. If not, you'll end up over-reacting and under-reacting.

Tim slammed on the brakes. The

tires squealed, and he barely missed being rear-ended by the driver behind him.

The driver honked angrily, then shot around him and sped off.

Dee was in the passenger seat, recovering from the shock. "Wha-at was that about? Why did you stop like that?"

"I saw a squirrel dart out onto the road," Tim said as he put the car back in gear. "I didn't want to hit it."

"A squirrel? You put our lives in danger and almost caused a car accident because of a squirrel? Next time, measure the importance of an injury to a squirrel versus the importance of injuries to you, me, and the driver behind us."

Over-reacting or Under-reacting?

_____ You're lost in the city. You whip out your phone and call 911.

_____ You're lost in the city. You hardly notice and just keep on walking in the same direction.

_____ A small child suddenly darts onto the road. You keep driving, assuming the child will realize there's a car coming and get off the road.

_____ A small child is on the sidewalk watching you drive toward her. You swerve wildly to get out of the way.

_____ A tornado warning comes over the radio. You go outside to see if one is really coming.

_____ A thunderstorm warning comes over the radio. You run down to the tornado shelter for the night.

Making mountains out of molehills

The expression *Don't make a mountain out of a molehill* is about over-reacting. When you make a mountain out of a molehill, you're magnifying the size of a problem. You see it bigger than it really is.

If you're the type of person who worries a lot, then knowing what's a big deal (and what's a small deal) is important. You don't want to get too upset by things that don't really matter.

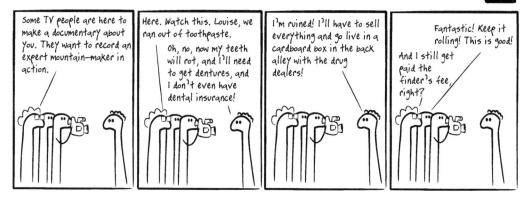

Are You a Mountain-maker?

_____ People tell you that you over-react to everything.

_____ You feel that many things are dangerous, especially things you don't understand.

_____ Every problem seems unsolvable.

_____ Other people move past obstacles in their lives more quickly than you do.

_____ People tell you you're dramatic, emotional, or a worrywort.

_____ When you're facing a problem, it usually seems so big that you don't know where to start.

Tips for mountain-makers

If you tend to worry a lot and don't know when you're making a mountain out of a molehill, here are some tests you can try.

- **The six-month test:** Ask yourself *How much will this matter six months from now?* If the answer is *not much* or *not at all*, then it's a molehill.

What to do

1 **Ask yourself if it will matter in six months.**
If not, don't sweat it.

2 **Ask yourself if you just feel like complaining.**
Sometimes that's all it is.

3 **Ask yourself what you're really worried about.**
Once you name it, you can decide if it really is a big deal.

■ **The complaining test:** Ask yourself *Do I just feel like complaining? Am I in a complaining mood?* Sometimes your mood makes you feel like making a fuss.

■ **The worry test:** Ask yourself *What exactly do I feel worried about?* Identify what you're afraid of and measure it using the big deal ruler. Maybe your feelings of worry are bigger than the thing you're worrying about.

"I'm worried about the menu for the

dinner party tomorrow. Should I serve applesauce with the pork chops? Or go with something less traditional? Will my guests like what I serve?" Meg pulled her hair. "Argh! I'm going crazy here! I can't even sleep at night!"

"Put it in perspective," her sister suggested. "Tell me: How much is all of this going to matter six months from now?"

Meg thought for a moment. "Not at all, really."

"Now ask yourself: What exactly are you worried about?"

Meg was silent. "I'm worried that I won't look classy in front of my classy friends."

"Now measure that on the big-deal ruler. Does it really matter if they think you're classy?"

"Not really," Meg answered. "Really, what I care about is that everybody has fun. Okay, that puts it all in perspective!"

Making molehills out of mountains

If you're the type of person who acts impulsively and forgets to do things, then you probably make molehills out of mountains. You see everything as a small deal.

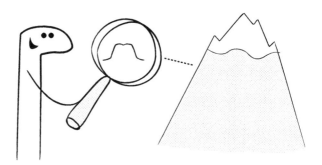

Are You a Molehill-maker?

_____ People tell you that you don't take things seriously enough.

_____ You usually ignore risks. Sometimes you find that risky things are kind of fun and exciting.

_____ You dislike thinking about big problems. You prefer to just think about something else.

_____ Other people talk about problems that don't bother you at all.

_____ People tell you you're absent-minded or irresponsible.

_____ You tell yourself that things really aren't worth worrying about.

Tips for molehill-makers

If you tend to disregard things and find out too late that it was important or dangerous, here are some tests you can try.

- **The worst-case test:** Ask yourself *What is the worst thing that can happen here?* If it's fairly bad, then don't wait to find out if it's actually going to happen. Get yourself out of the situation.

- **The fun test:** Ask yourself *Am I choosing the option that's the most fun, rather than the most important? Am I ignoring facts because I want things to be fun?* Sometimes your mood and appetite for fun can trick you into making a molehill out of a mountain.

4. Catastrophizing

Catastrophizing means making the biggest possible mountain out of every molehill. When you catastrophize, you see every problem as end-of-the-world doom.

Catastrophizing is a habit. Catastrophizers expect disaster at every turn. They believe that things are a lot worse than they actually are. They predict failure. They magnify tiny problems into terrifying situations.

Catastrophizers are often perfectionists who believe life should be perfect. And when it's not, they think it's a disaster.

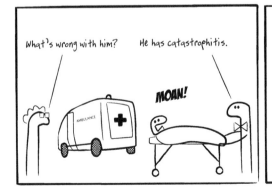

What catastrophizers catastrophize about:

- **Failure:** When catastrophizers fail at something, they assume it means they'll fail at everything. They expand one failure to cover everything. They never consider just fixing the mistake, learning from it, or trying something else.

- **Mistakes:** Catastrophizers are often perfectionists—they can't tolerate mistakes in themselves or others. So when they make a mistake, they take it too hard. Their over-reaction gets in the way of fixing the mistake, apologizing, and trying again.

- **Relationships:** Catastrophizers are over-sensitive about their relationships and are always looking for something going wrong. They over-react to small problems. Because they believe these problems are signs of failure, they don't even try to fix them. They don't consider that all relationships have problems, but most people talk them out.

People expect

... that a catastrophe is truly catastrophic.

They get annoyed if you're always catastrophizing about ordinary things.

"Hi, Don. Listen. I'm going to go

out with the girls tonight, so maybe we can go out on another night. See ya!"

Don clicked off the phone, feeling as if he'd been sucker-punched. Leah didn't want to go out with him.

The relationship was over. She didn't want to spend time with him anymore.

In fact, she hated him. She despised him.

And he'd never get another girlfriend. He'd be alone and lonely forever.

"You okay, Don?" his friend Luke asked.

"No," Don mumbled at his shoes. "Leah's gone out with the girls."

"Great! Then you can come out with us tonight!"

Don looked up. "Don't you get it? She's dumping me!"

"She said that?"

"No, but she's going out with the girls, so that's what it means."

"Seriously, stop with the catastrophizing. Unless she says she's dumping you, then she's not dumping you. Now get your coat. We're going, and you're coming!"

Making catastrophes happen

One problem with catastrophizing is that by believing catastrophic conclusions, you can end up making catastrophes happen. Instead of doing things to stop the problem from getting worse, you just wait and let it happen. This ends up turning a small incident into a big mistake.

Catastrophizing can become a never-ending cycle. The catastrophizer becomes negative and depressed and stops trying. That ends up creating catastrophes. The catastrophizer takes this as proof that his/her catastrophizing was correct in the first place. This makes him/her even more negative and depressed and ready to believe that the next tiny problem is a catastrophe.

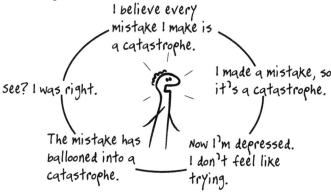

Louise had a bad month for sales.

She catastrophized about it, believing that it meant she was a lousy salesperson and that her career was over.

Her catastrophizing made her feel depressed. This made her behave differently with her clients. Now instead of being enthusiastic and outgoing, she was anxious and quiet. This scared off a lot of clients.

As a result, Louise ended up with even fewer sales the next month.

"See?" she wailed to her friends. "This just proves that my career is over!"

Louise never considered that it might have just been one slow month and by catastrophizing, she made the situation worse.

You can predict

1 **Over-reacting to small problems turns them into big problems.**
Catastrophizing make scatastrophes happen.

2 **People will get fed up if you catastrophize.**
They will start criticizing you to get you to solve your problems.

Al made a few mistakes at work.

He catastrophized about the situation and became terrified that if his boss found out, he'd fire Al. So instead of dealing with the problems and fixing them, he tried to hide them from his boss.

Eventually the boss discovered the mistakes. He was so angry with Al for trying to hide them that he put him on probation.

Ironically, it was Al's efforts to hide the mistakes that got him in trouble, not the mistakes themselves. Had he just fixed the mistakes and explained everything to the boss in the first place, his job would still be secure.

Don catastrophized when Leah,

his girlfriend, decided to go out with the girls. He magnified the situation until he believed that she was dumping him.

This belief made him act differently the next time he saw her. He was grouchy and negative. Sometimes he was accusing. They got into arguments over nothing.

So Leah got fed up with his negativity and dumped him.

Tips to stop the catastrophizing habit

- **Write down your thoughts:** Catastrophizing usually happens when you're alone and nobody's around to challenge your illogical beliefs. So write them down on paper. Include your predictions.

> I failed a test. I'm a failure.
> Prediction: I'll never get into college.

- **Argue with yourself:** Read what you wrote and start arguing with yourself. *No, that's not true...*

No, that's not true. Failing a test doesn't mean no college, or most students would never get into college.

- **Ask yourself "what if" questions:** Ask questions to force yourself to think of solutions. *What if I tried something else instead?*

- **Use perspective:** Measure your problem with the Big Deal Ruler. A small problem usually needs just a small solution. For example, one mistake isn't enough to cost you your job, especially if you fix the problem.

  Failing a test is a small-to-medium problem. It needs a small-to-medium solution.

- **Make new predictions:**
  Once you've eliminated your overblown predictions, make some more realistic predictions. What is most likely to happen? How will you handle it? Make a plan.

  I failed a test. I'm not perfect. I need to solve this problem.
  New prediction: My grade will drop 4%. If I get advice from the teacher, I can still make sure I get into college.

What to do

1 **Write it down.**
You'll understand more when you see it on paper.

2 **Argue with yourself.**
Pretend you're someone else.

3 **Ask what-if questions.**
Imagine different scenarios.

4 **Get perspective.**
Measure each scenario.

5 **Revise your predictions.**
Now you have things in perspective.

- **Make the best of your situation:** Sometimes there's no quick fix. The best you can do is learn from the mistake so that you don't make it again. Can you change how you do things to prevent this from happening in the future?

- **Laugh at yourself:** There's an old expression: *Happy are the people who laugh at themselves. They'll never cease to be amused.* Days or weeks from now, once the problem has blown over, you'll be able to look back on the problem and laugh at yourself. Everyone goofs up sometimes. Mishaps become great stories that you can tell people later on, especially when everyone is sharing their Most Embarrassing Moment stories.

- **Remember that virtually all problems can be solved:** There are very few unsolvable problems. If you take some time to think, you'll find a solution.

Are You a Catastrophizer?

_____ I feel anxious and scared a lot of the time.

_____ I believe before I start something that I'll probably fail.

_____ When I can't tell how bad something is, I believe that means it's really, really bad.

_____ People tell me that I over-react.

_____ In my mind, I always go through the worst-case scenarios.

_____ When obstacles come up in my life, I give up instead of trying to work around them.

_____ I feel that other people have an easier life than I do.

Summary

Perspective is like a ruler. It helps you measure how big, important, or risky something is. Whenever you're in a new situation, it's important to get perspective:

■ **Ask "how much" questions:** This helps you measure the importance of the situation. *How much do I need to react? How much will it cost? How much time will it take?*

■ **Use the "big deal" ruler:** Once you've got some perspective, measure it to figure out if this situation is a big deal. If it is, you need to respond. If it's not, then you can stop worrying about it.

■ **Compare big deals and bigger deals:** Sometimes you have to prioritize one important choice over another. Long-term big deals are bigger than short-term big deals. Big deals for other people are more important than big deals for you. And big deals regarding health and survival are more important than other big deals.

■ **Beware of over- and under-reacting:** When you don't have perspective, you'll end up over-reacting or under-reacting to a situation. You'll end up making mountains out of molehills or molehills out of mountains.

■ **Avoid catastrophizing:** Catastrophizing means turning a problem into a disaster. Virtually all problems can be solved.

CHAPTER 5
Motives

"Hey!"

Jed whirled around. Something had hit his head. He saw a wad of paper on the floor. But if anyone behind him had thrown it, they weren't showing it on their faces.

"What's up?" his friend Tim asked.

"Someone threw this at me for no reason!" Jed growled, tossing the wad into the garbage.

"Well, not for no reason," Tim said. "Everybody has a reason for everything they do."

"Even for this?"

Tim shrugged. "You're assuming one of the guys did it to tease you. But maybe it was some girl who likes you and wants to get your attention."

Jed hadn't thought of that. He glanced back again to see if there were any girls behind him, but if there had been any, they were gone now.

What is a motive?

Why do people do the things they do? Everyone always has a reason for their actions. That reason comes from their thoughts or feelings. It's invisible to other people, but there are clues that can help you figure it out.

A motive is like a flame inside a person. Think of the flames inside a motor. The heat from those flames makes the motor move, which makes the machine do something. You can't see the flame, but you can figure out from the actions that something inside is heating it up. A motive is like this kind of flame.

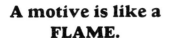

A motive is like a FLAME.

The flame is hidden inside people, fueling their actions and choices.

I want revenge

I want attention

But motives heat up body language, so that someone watching can get a whiff of the person's motive.

<sniff>

I'm trying to impress you

What can you get a whiff of? Often it's just a vague sense that something's unusual.

She's acting weird.

<sniff>

I'm jealous

Or maybe it's a sense that someone isn't telling the truth.

Why do I not believe you?

I'm tricking you.

When you know the motive, you know what fuels the behavior.

1. Motives and intentions

A motive is a reason why someone does something. It's usually some kind of goal or intention. That motive is the flame that causes their behavior. No motive means no behavior. You can often see motives in someone's body language.

serious face

straining muscles

tense body

I want to win!

Sometimes people tell you their motives. For example, a police detective might say, "I'm going to get to the bottom of this case!" Now you know the motive for his/her actions.

Sometimes people deliberately show you their motive through their facial expressions and body language. For example, a person who's trying to impress you might use big words and pretend to be smart.

trying to look smart

using big words

dropping famous names

I want to impress you!

But often people don't tell you or show you their motives. Sometimes they don't even realize themselves why they're doing things.

"Why is he doing that?" Ana asked.

"Probably no reason," Jim answered, still watching the little boy having his tantrum. "Kids don't know what they're doing."

"Everyone always has a motive for their actions. What do you think his might be?"

"He might want to let out his frustrations," Jim offered.

"Yes. Or he might be trying to get attention."

People assume

.. . that you can read their motives and intentions.

They assume you know what they know.

Figuring out motives

Watching someone's actions and listening to someone's words isn't enough to tell you his/her motives. For any action, there can be many possible motives.

Consider all the possible motives for a person who steals some food:

- **greed** (*I don't want to spend my money*)

- **compulsion** (*I have a psychiatric disorder*)

- **hunger** (*I haven't eaten in two days*)

- **fear** (*My gang is pressuring me*)

People expect

... that you'll take some time to figure out their real motives.

They get offended if you just assume the worst.

Figuring out motives is like trying to pick up the "scent" of the motive flame. It means watching body language and looking for unusual actions, expressions, and gestures.

Tips for figuring out someone's motive

- **Be curious.** Don't assume you already know why someone is doing something. Be prepared to learn new things about your friends.

What to do

1 **Be curious.**
Take some time to think.

2 **Collect evidence.**
Find behavior that points at one motive.

3 **Revise your first guesses.**
First guesses are often wrong.

4 **Question assumptions.**
Stereotypes get in the way.

5 **Watch for body language.**
It should match the context and the motive.

■ **Collect evidence:** Look for body language hints about the motive. For example, if someone's motive for stealing food is fear, then he/she will communicate fear through his/her body language, facial expressions, and movements. He/she may also communicate fear through words. Look for actions, body language, facial expressions, choices, and language that all point toward one motive.

■ **Revise your first guess:** If the actions you see don't match your first guess at the motive, then you probably need to revise it. Often the most likely motive isn't the right one.

Why is Jim mowing Anne's lawn?

Maybe he thinks she can't do it, so he's helping her. But she works out at the gym, so that can't be right.

Maybe she's paying him. She's been very busy lately. But she doesn't have a lot of money, so that's not very likely.

Maybe he likes her and he's trying to impress her. She does have a boyfriend, but I heard it's not going well. Maybe Jim's trying to make his move.

- **Question your assumptions:** Assumptions are like little conclusions that you've made long before you arrived at this situation. Some assumptions are right, but some are wrong. For example, you may assume that people usually have evil motives. If you do, then you'll be prejudiced to believe that their motives are bad, even if they're good.

- **Consider the context:** Context is like the fuel for motives. You can often figure out someone's motive if you think about the context and the person's body language at the same time. What's going on around him/her? What just happened or is about to happen? What expressions are on the person's face? What is he/she looking at? The motive connects body language to the context.

BODY LANGUAGE

MOTIVE

CONTEXT

You can predict

1 **Does the person's body language show any emotions?**
Those are clues about his/her motive.

2 **What clues are there in the context?**
Motive + Context = Actions

- **Consider the personality and culture.** Personality and culture affect a person's motive. People see things differently, so they react differently.

"I'd like a one-way flight to Tokyo,

please," Mary said, hoping the Japanese airline clerk spoke English.

The clerk smiled. "Perhaps you'd like to take the train."

Mary frowned. He must have misunderstood. "No, please, one ticket. I'd like to fly."

"There are many other ways to get there. It would be difficult to fly."

Mary was confused. What was he doing?

Later, she learned that in Japanese culture, it's considered rude for a customer service clerk to say no. The clerk was doing his best to let her know that there were no more flight tickets available.

- **Follow the money.** Money is a big motivator. But it's not always obvious who's getting paid to do things. Often money is a hidden motive. Always ask yourself if someone might be making money, and try to find out if they are.

- **Consider the person's role.** Most jobs and roles have built-in motives. Maybe someone's job is to help. Maybe it's to sell. Maybe it's to make you feel afraid of them. If the person is on the job, then their professional motive is probably their real motive at the moment.

A player was injured! I watched

the coach's reaction from the sidelines,. He didn't say anything, but he looked angry that the kid had gotten injured! Maybe he thought the kid wasn't careful enough.

But a few minutes later I overheard him. "Wow, I feel really bad. She's going to the hospital. This could affect her whole season. I feel responsible."

Did I ever get the motive wrong! Here I was thinking he was blaming the kid for getting injured, when, in fact he was feeling somehow responsible for it.

Facial expressions can be hard to read all by themselves. Sometimes you have look at the context and the person's job to figure out their real motive.

What to do

1 **Consider personality and culture.**
Sometimes manners and mannerisms are just different from yours.

2 **Follow the money.**
Money is a big motivator.

3 **Consider jobs and roles.**
Responsibilities have a lot to do with motives, especially in the workplace..

What's the Motive?	
Action	**Motive**
I go to work every day, even though I don't like my job.	Money
A bored child has a loud temper tantrum.	_____
I make a special cake for my girl/boyfriend's birthday.	_____

You can prioritize

1 **Considering all the facts**
...is more important than...

2 **Getting to an answer quickly.**

2. Misreading motives

It's easy to misread motives. You can't see the flame fueling someone's actions. The best you can do is guess, based on all the evidence. But this doesn't mean you should just jump to conclusions.

Racing to get to "Because"

When you're trying to figure out someone's motive, you're asking a lot of *Why* questions. *Why is he doing that? Why are his actions so stiff? Why is his voice higher than usual?*

Sometimes you just can't wait to get to *Because*. It feels good to solve a mystery and get an answer. Quick answers make you feel safe and knowledgeable.

Except that quick answers are often *wrong*.

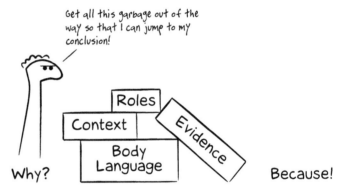

If you try to get an answer too fast, you can end up jumping to conclusions.

"Don't listen to them. They're just

gossiping," Kate told Meg, taking her aside.

"Why do you say it's gossip?" Meg asked.

"Because they have only bits and pieces of information. Little things they saw, other things they overheard. And they've pieced them all together to figure out what people are up to."

"They jump to conclusions, you mean."

"Yes. They think they have enough information to guess at people's intentions and motives. But they don't. And they end up spreading lies."

How to avoid misreading motives

- **Be skeptical of the first idea that pops into your head.** The first thing that pops into your head is like a lazy detective who shows up, glances around, says he's solved the mystery, and demands to be paid so he can leave. This first detective is extremely unreliable.

- **Look for counter-evidence.** Avoid the temptation to just look for evidence that supports what you already think. Look for evidence that proves you're wrong. That will help you find the true answer.

■ **Correct your errors.** Rigid thinking, or trying to always be right, is a problem for figuring out motives. Accept that your first conclusions are probably wrong. Keep revising them as you get new information.

"I think Louise wants to break up

with me," Ted moaned.

"Why do you think that?" his friend Jake asked.

"Why? Because she hasn't been around much lately, and when she is, she's irritable!"

"It's not a good idea to believe the first thing that pops into your head," Jake cautioned. "It's likely to be wrong. Instead, look for counter-evidence. Are there any other reasons why she might be busy or irritable?"

"Well, she has a big project at work. I know she's been up late working on it."

"That could be it," Jake said. "Why don't you call her and ask how her work is going? That'll allow you two to talk about the amount of time you're not spending together."

What to do

1 **Be wary of the first thing that pops into your head.**
It's often wrong.

2 **Look for counter-evidence.**
Try to disprove your theories.

3 **Revise and correct.**
Don't cling to wrong conclusions.

List Some Possible Motives	
Action	**Possible Motives**
Your friend Ted sells his car and starts biking every-where. He tells you it's because he wants to get in shape.	He wants to get in shape (as he said). He wants to save money. He wants to impress a girl he likes. He wants to train for a race.
You see a man hit another man with a heavy briefcase.	_____ _____ _____ _____

3. Miscommunicating your motives

You may be surprised at what people think your your motives and intentions are. They may conclude that you're being mean when you were trying to be kind. They may conclude you're being careless on purpose, when really you were trying your best.

How does this happen? First, the other person could mis-read your motives But more important, you could miscommunicate them.

How you miscommunicate your motives

■ **You assume others know what you mean, so you don't explain.** People can't read your mind. You have to show or tell them your intentions.

People expect

... that you'll communicate your intentions clearly.
If they misunderstand, it's your fault for communicating poorly.

■ **You let your body language contradict your thoughts and words.** Less than 10 percent of your message comes from your words. The rest comes from your body language and voice. Make sure that your facial expressions, gestures, and voice say the same thing as you're saying.

"Why is everybody angry with me?"

Sam was bewildered. Just a few minutes ago, everything was going fine. Now suddenly nobody wanted to talk to him.

"Jess just confessed to everyone that she'd made that horrible mistake in last week's report," Meg explained. "But you didn't say anything."

"So? What was there to say?"

"Something reassuring. But you just stood there, looking silent and cold. Everyone assumed you were disapproving. They assumed from your body language that you were blaming her."

"But I wasn't blaming her! I didn't even say anything! In fact, I was thinking about something else."

"Your body language and silence said things for you," Meg said. "Things would have gone more smoothly if you'd said something nice out loud."

■ **You do things that suggest other motives.** For example, if you decide to argue with someone, you communicate that you're self-centered, that you believe you're more important than anyone else, and that you intend to force your opinion on others. Maybe all you were trying to do was join the conversation in a friendly way. Your actions didn't communicate that. Avoid actions that contradict your intentions.

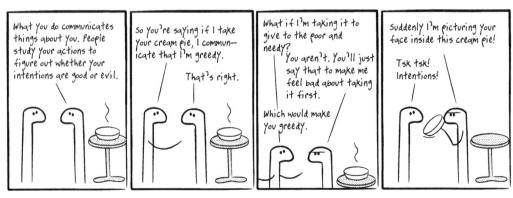

How Might Someone Misinterpret Your Motive?

Action	Misinterpreted Motive
Rob's girlfriend Maya sees him eating with Tina. He's trying to be nice because Tina forgot her lunch.	Maya might think Rob's interested in Tina.
Everyone decides to go to the movies. Lily doesn't want to go, so she doesn't say anything.	

4. How to tell when someone is lying

Is it easy to tell if someone is lying? It turns out that it is very difficult. Police and court judges have years of professional training and experience dealing with liars. Yet research has shown that they are no better than the average person at figuring out who is lying.

However, there are still several body language, communication, and behavior clues that can give you a whiff of the intention to lie to you.

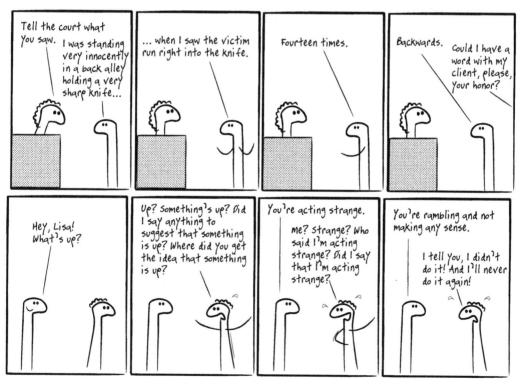

All actors are really professional liars—they've learned how to create the illusion that they're telling the truth. But most people think they're better actors than they really are.

Here are some clues that someone is lying to you.

Body language clues

- **Forced smile.** A liar often smiles while talking to you, but the smile doesn't look real. It looks more like stretched lips or a half-laugh. A natural smile pushes the top of the cheeks upward, so there are usually crinkles around the eyes. A forced smile is only in the lips. The eyes are still round.

- **Touching the mouth.** Liars often touch their mouth while talking, such as touching their lips. This is a subconscious gesture. You can think of it as the hand trying to push the lying words back into the mouth.

- **Mismatched body language.** If someone says "I love that shirt" without smiling or looking happy, then that is a mismatch. If someone says "I missed the train" but doesn't look sad, worried, or disappointed, then that is a mismatch. Believe the body language, not the words.

Speech clues

- **Lack of contractions.** A liar tends to use full words (*will not, cannot*) instead of contractions (*won't, can't*). Example: "*I did not do it*" instead of "*I didn't do it.*"

- **Repetition.** A liar tends to repeat your words back to you. Example: You ask, "*Did you steal my pen?*" and they reply "*No, I did not steal your pen*" instead of "*No, I didn't*" or just "*No.*"

- **Truth phrases.** A liar uses truth phrases, such as "*To tell the truth*" or "*To be honest.*" Why? The person is stalling while searching for the right words. They're also trying to overstate their case.

People assume

... that overstating a lie makes it easier to believe.
But overstatement is a clue that it's a lie.

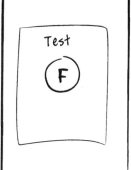

- **Indirect answers.** Liars don't answer questions with a direct answer. They choose their words carefully so that they don't actually give an answer.

- **Long answers.** Liars usually have to make up the details while they're talking. For this reason, they tend to include a lot of details that aren't necessary. False answers tend to be long, rambling, and repetitious. True answers tend to be short and straightforward.

What to do

1 **Look for body language clues.**
Forced smiles, touching the mouth, and mismatched body language are clues that someone is lying.

2 **Listen for speech clues.**
Liars overstate their case or use extra formal language.

3 **Look for clues in the context.**
Observe what's going on around you for evidence.

Context clues

■ **Check the people around you.** Are people nearby trying not to snicker? Are they smiling too much and exchanging glances, as if they're enjoying a joke? Are close friends looking concerned and trying to signal to you? These are signs that someone is lying to you and that everybody else knows.

■ **Check the objects around you.** Is there anything in the context that doesn't make sense with what the person is saying? You may need to glance behind the person if he/she is trying to hide something from your eyes.

■ **Think about the past.** Did anything happen recently that might make this person lie to you? Is anything about to happen that might make the person lie? What memories and experiences do you have with this person?

Eye contact clues

Do people look you in the eye when they are lying?

Sometimes they do. But *too much eye contact* is a big clue that the person is lying.

Eye contact isn't about staring at someone's eyes. It's about searching the face near the eyes for small changes in expression.

In real eye contact, the person's eyes flit around your face and look as if they're searching. Their eye contact is mildly curious.

Did his smile deepen? Are his eyes crinkling? But look, he's smiling less now, and his eyes look more serious...

In contrast, liars either stare at your face as if they're doing fake eye contact, or they look at your face as if they're checking to see if you believe what they're saying.

Basically, their eye contact is too intense to be natural.

Of course I'll pay you for it.

Is she lying? She's making steady eye contact... but she's just looking at my eyes. Her eyes aren't flitting around my face.

And it feels as if she's staring and grinning at me. She looks a bit like a maniac.

Sorry, no deal.

Rats. What gave me away?

Showing your fangs when you tried to fake the eye contact.

Also, eye contact at the wrong time is another sign that someone is lying. When people are truly searching their memory for information, they tend to look off into space, usually up over your shoulder. It looks as if they're trying to visualize the event in their memory.

Well, I remember it was raining that night...

Someone who's just making up a story will look you in the eye. They won't gaze off into space. This is a clue that they're not really searching their memory.

So if someone is still looking at your face while trying to describe a memory, suspect that the person is lying.

People assume

... that strong eye contact is always linked with telling the truth.

But for remembering, people need to look off into space to visualize their memories.

"Did you take my laptop?"

The guys were always playing practical jokes. Tim found jokes annoying. But he knew that if he got angry, they'd tease him for that. So he kept his voice calm and watched closely to see if they were lying.

"No, to be honest, we did not," Paul answered, making extremely direct eye contact.

The others snickered silently behind him.

"We were just sitting here, doing nothing, honestly," Ted explained. "And your laptop was right there. And then Tina came in and started talking to us..." He rambled on for a long while. "...And that is the truth of what really happened."

"Really," Tim responded. "Let me rephrase the question, then, because you're such lousy liars. Is my laptop in Ted's locker?"

There was a pause.

"No," Ted said suddenly. He gave an odd frown and waved his hands toward his locker. "How could it be in there?"

Tim sighed as if bored. "Because that's where you put it last time. You guys are so predictable. Get it for me, and I'll buy us some fries."

Who's Probably Lying?

_____ The man's eyes widened as if he were offended. "Of course not! How dare you accuse me! I did not steal anything! And that is the truth!"

_____ While answering your question about what happened last night, the woman gazed over your shoulder, as if she was trying to visualize what she remembered.

_____ While answering your question about what happened last week, the man met your gaze steadily and gave quick replies.

_____ When you asked if he'd taken your shoes, the boy talked fast. You noticed he was shoving a shoelace into his pocket.

_____ "Of course I got it done," your project partner said. But he was frowning. The last time he said that in that way, he didn't have anything done at all.

_____ "No, I didn't!" she said. "I wasn't even there." The people around her nodded, looking from her to you.

Summary

A motive is the reason why a person does the things he/she does. A motive is like a flame that fuels actions and body language.

Figuring out someone's motive can be challenging, especially if you don't know the person very well. But you can improve your chances of getting it right by following these guidelines:

- **Don't believe the first thing that pops into your head.**

- **Look for evidence and counter-evidence.**

- **Correct your errors and assumptions.**

Misreading someone's intentions often results from jumping to conclusions. Never be in a rush to get an answer about someone's intentions. Spend time observing and gathering evidence.

Remember that other people are trying to figure out your motives. Here are some ways to avoid giving people the wrong message:

- **Say it.** Don't assume that people know what you mean. When you leave things unsaid, people use their imagination and guess.

- **Beware of your body language.** Make sure that your body language matches your intentions.

- **Avoid sending out contradictory messages.** Focus on communciating your intention, and make sure everything you do reinforces it.

Learn the telltale signs that someone is lying:

- **Body language clues:** the forced smile, touching the mouth, and mismatched body language

- **Speech clues:** lack of contractions, repetition, truth phrases, indirect answers, and long answers

- **Context clues:** the people around you, the objects around you, and events in the recent past

- **Eye contact clues:** too much or too little eye contact

CHAPTER 6
Decisions

Should she choose all advanced

courses? Or should she take some easy ones too?

Shen growled and nearly crumpled up the course selection form. She'd been staring at it for an hour, arguing with herself.

Hard courses were good. That's what gets you into good colleges. And her grades were fine. But how bad would the workload be? She couldn't afford to see her grades drop.

One or two easy courses would be fun. But would she get bored? And would they not count at all on a college application?

Every time she asked someone to help her make this decision, they always told her it was her own decision.

Great. What they didn't realize is that decisions were like torture.

And if she didn't figure out what to choose pretty soon, she was going to be bald from ripping her hair out.

What is a decision?

A decision is like a knife that pierces an escape hole. You're stuck in a dilemma, and you need to find the way out. Your decision knife has to be sharp, so you can aim well and make a clear cut.

Decisions improve when you use common sense. Never do the first thing that pops into your head. That's usually just a feeling. Good decisions are based on careful consideration of all the possibilities.

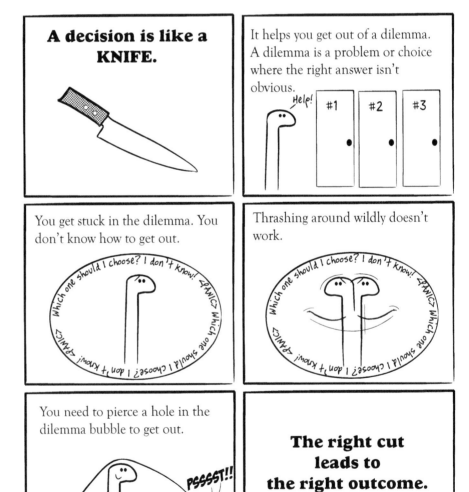

1. Dilemma bubbles

A dilemma is a problem with no obvious solution. At least once a day, you'll find yourself stuck in a dilemma. Not being able to make a decision feels like being stuck. You simply don't know what to do.

If you find decisions bewildering, it's probably because something is clouding your decisions. You can't really see what's on the other side.

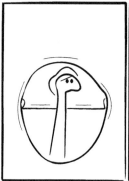

Types of dilemma bubbles:

■ **Perfectionism:** Perfectionists want everything exactly right all the time. They have a mental picture in their head of how things are supposed to be, and they get can't cope when reality doesn't turn out that way. When there's no perfect solution to a dilemma, they can't see any solution at all. Perfectionism is a big barrier to making decisions, because in real life, there's never a perfect choice. There's just a choice that happens to be better than the others.

- **Overwhelming options:** Sometimes you have to choose among many options. Which college should you go to? There are hundreds! What career should you choose? There are more than hundreds. Having so many options can be overwhelming. The task of narrowing your decision down to one choice seems impossible.

- **Fear of change:** Decisions almost always require you to change. If you choose this college, then that means you'll be leaving home to live in a different city. If you choose this boyfriend, then you have to adapt to being in a relationship. If you're afraid of change, then you'll run away from making big decisions. Sometimes big changes can be scary. When the choices are scary, some people can't make a decision.

You can predict

1 **People who are afraid of change will avoid making decisions.**
They don't really want to get out of their dilemma bubble.

2 **People with too many options sometimes hide from making decisions.**
They can't cope with too much information.

3 **Perfectionists rarely make good decisions.**
They're too afraid of making a mistake.

■ **Opportunity costs:** When you make a decision and choose one option, that means you walk away from all the other options. If you choose College A, then you don't get any of the nice features of College B or C. By choosing, you give up the other options.

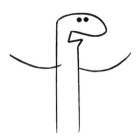

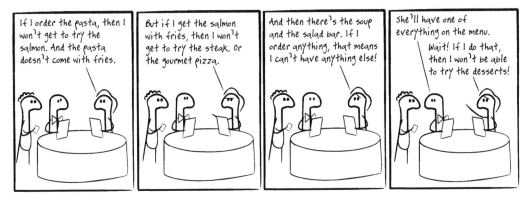

But all decisions have opportunity costs, and all decisions open new doors while they close other doors. Focusing on what you lose gets in the way of seeing what you'll gain.

- **Emotion bubbles:**
  Sometimes you're capable of making a decision, but your emotions stand in the way. Are you angry or resentful about the decision? Is it about something you hate? Strong feelings about a decision can get in the way of tackling it.

I really resent choosing when someone tells me I have to choose.

Dan's mother's arms were folded
across her chest, and she looked ready to burst with annoyance.

"Just do as I told you!" she said again.

Dan struggled. Part of him wanted to do what his mom was telling him. But another part was refusing to cooperate. And right now, that second part was stronger.

"My body won't let me!" he cried finally. "I can't make it do it!"

"You just make yourself do it!"

"I can't! Something won't let me!"

Mom's frown suddenly faded. "That's pride, Dan. It's an emotion. Your emotions have put up a wall because you feel as if you're being pushed."

"I think you're right. I can't think. I can't do anything!"

"Emotions can get control of you if you're not careful. When you're making decisions, you need to tell your emotions to get out of the way. Otherwise, you'll make bad decisions."

What to do

1 **Resist perfectionism.**
Life isn't about being perfect.

2 **Reduce overwhelming options.**
Use the quick decision techniques discussed later in this chapter.

3 **Be aware of any fear of change.**
Emotions get in the way of decison making.

4 **Accept that life has opportunity costs.**
When you choose one thing, you can't have another.

5 **Beware of emotions.**
Anger and pride can make you refuse to choose.

What's the Dilemma?

Dilemma

_____ You can't decide what to wear for graduation, so you avoid shopping for clothes. Deep down, you don't want to deal with leaving your school and going to a new school.

_____ You can't choose a thesis and get started on your research paper. Nothing you come up with seems good enough.

_____ If you go to theater school, then you can't go to college.

_____ You stare at the list of 40 ice cream flavors, and your brain locks. You can't even think.

Dilemma Types

A. Perfectionism

B. Overwhelming options

C. Fear of change

D. Opportunity costs

E. Emotion bubbles

The challenge of dilemma bubbles

You can get stuck in a dilemma bubble if you fall into old patterns. These patterns aren't decisions. They aren't sharp like a knife, and they don't pierce the bubble. In fact, they usually make the dilemma worse.

- **Blanking, looping, and panicking:** Sometimes decisions can make your brain stop working. You can't think at all. You don't know how to get it working again. You stare at the options without knowing what to do. So you stare at them even more, which reminds you that you don't know what to do. You start to loop and panic.

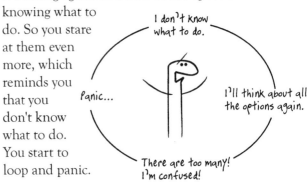

Karen stared at the menu, feeling

panic start to bubble inside her. There were four items she could order. But each one had something she liked and something she didn't like.

The others had already placed their order. They were all looking at her. The waitress was waiting, her pencil poised on her order pad.

Karen squeezed her eyes shut, then stared at the menu again. Now it was so blurry she couldn't even read it.

"I... I don't know... I... um..."

"Would you like me to come back in a few minutes?" the waitress said.

"Please," Karen whispered, relieved.

- **Ignoring the problem:** You don't like the decision, so you pretend it isn't there. You don't think about it at all... till it's too late to make a decision. But ignoring facts doesn't make them go away. The dilemma is still there: you're just doing nothing about it.

- **Waiting for perfect information:** You want the solution to be obvious. When it isn't, you tell yourself you don't have all the information you need to make the decision. But really, you're avoiding the decision because you don't know what to choose.

- **Procrastinating:** You put off making a decision till later, hoping the right answer will somehow fall into your lap in the meantime. But it never happens that way, and you never make a decision.

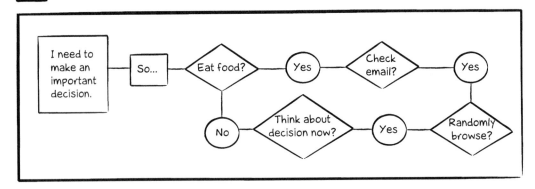

- **Choosing randomly:** When options are over-whelming, you might just close your eyes and pick one. You don't even care which one.

"Choose a novel for your book report,

and sign it out in the next fifteen minutes," the teacher said.

Tim stared at the walls and walls of books in the library. The colors seemed to blur.

He watched the other students drift toward the novel section. He followed, not sure what to do next.

He scanned the book spines of the shelf in front of him. The words were sideways, which annoyed his eyes. He pressed them closed, then tried tilting his head.

There were just too many books! How could anyone choose just one book from these thousands?

Tim closed his eyes again and randomly pulled one book off the shelf. Without even looking at it, he signed it out.

Unfortunately, on his way back to school, he discovered that it was a little kid's book on space aliens. He felt embarrassed even holding it.

2. How to make good decisions

These tips will help you make good decisions:

- **Decide what your goal is:** Having a clear goal helps you aim your decision knife.

- **Think about your priorities:** What's most important? Are some aspects bigger than others? What's going to matter most in the long run? Sort out your priorities before you try to make a decision.

- **See what other people are doing:** Get ideas from others. Look around. How are other people solving the problem? Often you can use the same solutions for your problems.

- **Collect information, but limit it:** There's no such thing as a perfect decision. You may feel that with a little more time and information, you can make a superb decision, but uncertainty is a part of life. Get comfortable with imperfect decisions. Make the decision with the best information you have right now.

You can prioritize

1 **Getting to a practical decision**
   ...is better than...

2 **Waiting for perfect information.**

What to do

1 **Focus on your goal.**
What do you want to accomplish?

2 **Prioritize.**
What's most important for this decision?

3 **Observe others.**
Learn to follow the decision techniques others use.

4 **Collect facts and information.**
But don't spend too much time on it.

5 **Make your decision.**

I can't decide which of these four books is the best one. Instead of wasting more time, I'll read the first paragraph of each and see which author catches my interest.

Tim returned the kid's book to the

library, determined to make a better decision this time.

He decided that his goal was to find a book that was interesting enough to hold his attention. He liked adventure and future fantasy books best. So he asked the librarian to show him how to find those books.

Then he considered his priorities. He had a lot of other homework, so he needed the book to be short enough to read in just a few days.

He looked for slim books with interesting titles. After a few minutes, he had a stack of ten books. Tim frowned. How could he narrow it down to one book?

He decided to base his decision on the back cover blurb. He'd take a first choice book and a spare, in case the first one turned out to be a dud.

Five minutes later, he walked out the library with two books in hand.

What Kind of Dilemma Bubble?

Actions

_____ You have to choose which play to go see. But you want the choice to be obvious, with no opportunity costs.

_____ You have to choose between starting now or waiting till later. Your mind darts back and forth between the two options while panic builds inside you.

_____ You need to choose a thesis for your essay. But you decide to do it tomorrow. The paper isn't due for another week anyway.

_____ You're confused about whether to go to college or not. So you pretend the application forms and deadlines don't even exist.

Bubble Types

A. Blanking and looping

B. Ignoring the problem

C. Waiting for perfect information

D. Procrastinating

E. Choosing randomly

3. Quick decision techniques

If you find decisions difficult and get stuck in dilemma bubbles, then you may need some decision-making techniques.

These techniques are easy tricks you can use whenever you have to make a decision.

Usually any one of these techniques can take you right to a final decision. But even when they don't, they get you thinking, and that helps you get out of the dilemma.

You can prioritize

1 Being able to make quick, practical, useful decisions about everyday things
   ...is more valuable than...

2 Being able to make perfect decisions.

1. Yum-yuck technique

The yum-yuck technique is useful when you have too many options and you need to eliminate some of them.

Line up your options. Point to each one, one after another, and quickly say either *yum* or *yuck*. This technique tests your instinctive reactions to your choices. Eliminate the yucks. Then go over the yums again, making some of them yucks. Eliminate those yucks.

Continue until you have just one yum left.

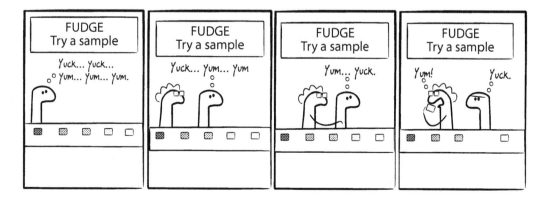

2. Simple-is-best technique

This technique works when you have to choose between two ideas. It's based on the principle that *The simplest plan is the best plan.*

Assess your plan options to figure out which one is the *least complicated.* Choose that one.

Why? Complex ideas with lots of cool angles work well only in our imaginations. They seldom work out in real life. The more parts there are, the more things can go wrong.

Choosing the simplest plan allows you to do one thing well, rather than several things badly.

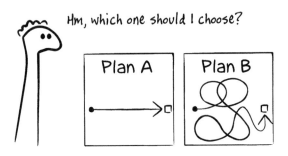

"No, let's do it really big!" Cat said.

"Instead of doing just one video, let's make a set of five videos, all on the same theme! That would be way better!"

"No, it wouldn't," her project partner said. "It would be too much. We're better off doing one video well than trying to do five of them and doing them badly."

"We can do it!" Cat argued. "We'll make it great! I can picture it!"

"Just because you can picture it, that doesn't mean we can do it. Simple is best. Let's do one thing really, really well."

3. Pop technique

This technique works really fast, but it's not a good technique for impulsive people who tend to give in to their whims. It works well for choosing research topics.

First look over your options. One will usually grab your attention more than the others. It seems to *pop* out.

Consider choosing the one that pops. It's often a good choice, because it's already interesting to you. You're more likely to stick with a topic that intrigues you, even if it's the hardest one.

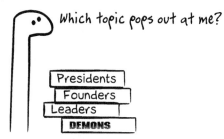

4. When-in-doubt-get-out technique

This technique is helpful when someone asks you to do something. Should you answer *yes* or *no*?

If you're not sure if you should do it, or you don't think you have the time, then you have doubts about saying yes. Saying yes when you have doubts is not a good idea.

Beware of saying yes just because someone requests something, or because you want to please others. Some people do this impulsively. You'll be angry with yourself later, and you'll do the request badly. That won't please anyone.

Get more information about what the request involves. If you feel you can do it, then accept. But if you still have doubts, politely explain that you don't think you have time.

"Will you help me move tomorrow?"

"Sure!" Jake said, without giving it a second thought.

"Great! Tomorrow morning at nine. See you!"

His friend Al drove off. Just then, Jake realized he had promised to help his dad cut down the hedge tomorrow morning.

He groaned. How did he get himself into these things? He was always saying yes too fast. It was as if he didn't ever want to let anybody down. He liked how helping people made him feel good.

Now he'd have to call Al back and say no. He cringed at the thought. Al would think he was a slacker. Would he even believe that Jake had to help his dad?

Maybe he should lie and say he broke his leg...

5. Road-less-traveled technique

Sometimes you have to choose between an easy option and a harder but more worthwhile option. The easy route is always tempting, but the harder route is usually better.

For example, it's harder to tell the truth and face someone's anger than it is to hide from the truth. It's harder to pay someone back what you owe than to pretend you didn't borrow it. And it's harder to select the hard course that will be helpful in your program than to sign up for the easy course that all your friends are taking.

First, look at your options. Rate one as Safe-Easy and the other as Hard-Worthwhile. Then choose the hard one.

You can prioritize

1 **Things that are challenging**
  ...are usually better than...

2 **Things that are too easy.**

6. What-would-Charlie-do technique

Is there someone you admire, a person who seems to make great decisions all the time? It can be a famous person or someone you know personally.

In this test, simply ask yourself: *What would that person do?* The answer will give you a good option.

Sometimes imagining someone else making a decision helps cut through a dilemma bubble.

7. Flip-a-coin technique

Heads or tails. Eenie-meenie-minie-moe. They're primitive techniques, but they work. However, use these last-resort techniques only after you've done other tests and are down to two or three equally good options, and you can't decide between them.

Flipping a coin is useful because it puts an end to the decision-making process. You don't waste time trying to come up with a perfect choice.

What's the Quick Decision Technique?

Decisions

_____ You know it would be easier to choose the short book, but the long book looks more interesting.

_____ You have to choose between two plotlines for your new novel. One has 12 main characters, and the other has three. You choose the one with three main characters.

_____ You don't know which job to choose. You imagine how famous people you admire would handle this decision.

_____ You have to choose whether or not to help your friend sell computers out of the back of his truck. Something doesn't seem right. You decide not to do it.

Techniques

A. Yum yuck

B. Simple is best

C. Pop test

D. When in doubt get out

E. The road less traveled

F. What would Charlie do

G. Flip a coin

People assume

... that you'll take big decisions seriously.

Quickie decision techniques are inappropriate for big decisions.

---

4. Big decisions

Some decisions are too big to make with quickie techniques.

You wouldn't choose which job to accept based on a flip of a coin. You wouldn't choose a college using yum-yuck.

Big decisions involve too much information to choose quickly. You have to write things down and think about them one at a time.

For some people, making big decisions is overwhelming, and they want the decision to just go away. But if you have some techniques for sorting out the information, you'll be able to make clear choices.

The decision tree technique

In a decision tree, you draw a tree trunk with branches and twigs to record and rate all the information that's important for your decision. Here's how to do it.

1. Draw a wide tree trunk with a few branches coming out from the top.

2. Write your dilemma on the trunk of the tree. It will be in the form of a question.

3. Write your choices on the branches.

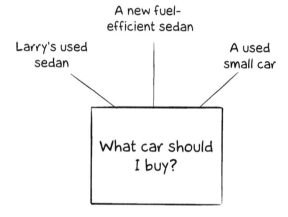

4. Draw a few twigs coming from each branch. On each twig, write an outcome or consequence for this option. Draw as many twigs as you need.

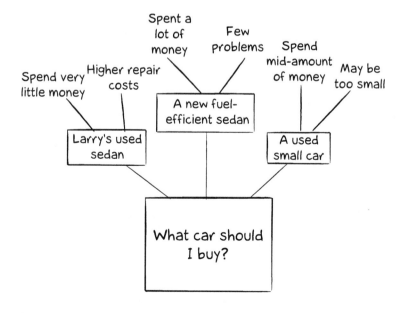

5. Rate each twig on a scale of –5 (very bad) to +5 (very good). Zero is neutral. Decide how good each outcome is for you.

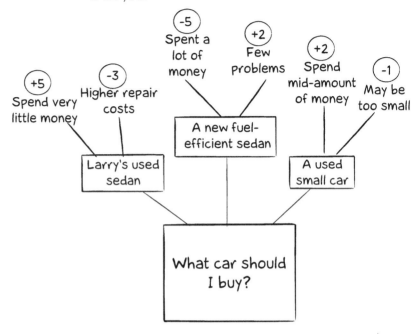

6. Add the numbers for each option. Which option has the best-rated outcomes? Which one has the worst-rated outcomes?

☆ Larry's used sedan: 5 - 3 = **2**
A new fuel-efficient sedan: 2 - 5 = **-3**
A used small car: 2 - 1 = **1**

4. Choose the best-rated option.

5. Ask friends for feedback. They may mention outcomes that you hadn't considered.

"I've been putting off this decision

for weeks. But the deadline is almost here. I have to choose my first, second, and third choices for my college application form."

Ana tried to think. She pressed her eyes closed and imagined the colleges she'd visited. Then she opened them and looked at the pamphlets and booklets.

Green's College had the best-rated programs, but it was far away, and the tuition was high. Smithson College was closer and had a decent reputation. And State College was the most economical with the shortest travel.

Which one to choose? Ana took out a piece of paper and drew up a decision tree.

Make a decision tree about Ana choosing a college. Some information is provided. You may have to imagine some of the details. Use short forms if the words get crowded. Add up the points at the bottom to see which one seems best.

Which College Would You Choose?

Green's College: very high tuition feeds, best-rated program, must fly to get there

Smithson College: medium tuition feeds, good program, one-day bus ride to get there

State College: low tuition fees, highly rated program, 30-minute bus ride to get there

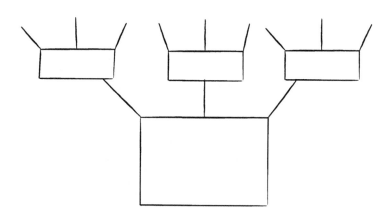

Green's College: _____

Smithson College: _____

State College: _____

5. Handling disappointment

Sometimes you don't get to do what you want. The option you'd really like isn't available. What do you do then?

Jena stared in disbelief at the clerk.

After spending half a day deciding which dress to buy for the prom, she learned that the dress of her choice was sold earlier that day.

"Can't you get in any more?" she cried.

"Not in time for the prom," the clerk said kindly. "But we do have plenty more dresses."

Jena just walked out of the store. She sat down on the curb and put her head on her arms.

She'd spent so long deciding! And now her choice was gone! How was she supposed to deal with that?

Life is full of these disappointments, so it's important to develop strategies for handling them. Here are a few ideas:

■ **When you can't do the thing you want, do the next-best thing.** People often don't get their first choice. But usually, the second choice is very good. What's important is to make sure you don't get stuck.

People expect

... that you'll adapt to the choices available to you.

Adapting to reality is part of life.

- **Sometimes life is trying to tell you something.** Sometimes your first choice isn't the right choice. You may think you know what to choose, but sometimes life chooses for you—and chooses better. There are always hidden opportunities in disappointments if you choose to look for them.

You can prioritize

1 **Getting on with your life**
...is better than...

2 **Getting stuck in disappointment.**

Ted remembered back in the spring,
when he'd received the rejection letter from college.

They'd turned him down flat. His grades were okay, but they were in the wrong subject areas. He needed more maths and sciences, and fewer dramas, arts, and literatures.

Ted's second choice, the quirky theater school in the next state, had sent him an acceptance the same day. But Ted was too upset to even consider going to his second choice.

But his dad encouraged him. "Somtimes life is trying to tell you something, son. Maybe you're not a scientist. Maybe you're supposed to be some kind of artist."

So reluctantly, Ted accepted.

Now eight months later, he recognized it as the best decision he'd ever made. Theater school was perfect for him. He was lucky that his first choice turned him down!

Summary

A decision is like a knife, because a dilemma is like a bubble. You need the knife to slice your way out of the bubble. Here are some of the things to consider when struggling with decisions:

- **Types of dilemma bubbles:** Recognize what kind of dilemma you're stuck in: perfectionism, overwhelming options, fear of change, opportunity costs, or emotion bubbles.

- **Challenges of dilemma bubbles:** Be aware what is happening in your mind while you're in a dilemma bubble. Are you looping and blanking? Ignoring the problem? Waiting for perfect information? Or just choosing randomly?

- **Steps in good decision-making:** Start by identifying your goal. What exactly are you trying to achieve? Then figure out your priorities. How important is this compared to other things going on in your life? Observe how others are handling the decision to get ideas for how you could handle it. Collect facts and information, but don't fall into the trap of looking for perfect information. Then choose based on the best information you have.

- **Quick decision techniques:** Use these techniques when you need to make a small decision quickly: the yum-yuck test, the simple-is-best test, the pop test, the when-in-doubt-get-out test, the road-less-traveled test, the what-would-Charlie-do test, and the flip-a-coin test.

- **The decision tree technique:** For bigger decisions, use a pencil and paper. Draw a decision tree showing all your choices and all the possible outcomes. Rate each one to help you measure the pros and cons.

- **Disappointment:** Sometimes you don't get your first choice. Instead of despairing, choose the next best option. Recognize that sometimes life makes choices for you, and often those choices are the best ones.

CHAPTER 7
Happiness

Jess watched the partygoers with
a pang of envy.

Everyone is happy except me, she thought resentfully. Everyone else has tons of friends and exciting places to go. They have cool clothes and great gear. Everybody knows them.

Meanwhile, I'm a nobody. I have exactly three friends. I never go anywhere except to a movie or to someone's house to play video games. And there's nothing exciting happening in my so-called life!

And here was yet another party that she wasn't even invited to. Never mind that it wasn't her sort of thing at all—she just wanted to be like everyone else.

She trudged home, went to her room, and closed the door.

"There's a phone message for you!" her mom called after her.

"I don't care," Jess mumbled to herself.

What is happiness?

Television gives us one image of happinessa—laughing, being rich, and having lots of friends, lots of stuff, and a life of endless pleasure and perfection. But the truth is that many TV people aren't happy at all. So that means happiness is something else entirely.

Real happiness is like an elastic band. It stretches and adapts to reality, making you feel calm and content. It helps you find happiness inside yourself instead of in things that don't matter.

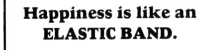

Happiness is like an ELASTIC BAND.

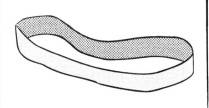

Happiness stretches to fit situation, especially bad times. Because it stretches, it doesn't break.

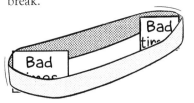

It can reach far around things and hold them together, then relax back into its regular shape.

Happiness is not a feeling. It's not a smily-face.

Happiness is a sense of your own strength. It makes you feel peaceful and gives you joy just being alive.

Happiness is something you learn.

1. Resilience

Resilience means being able to bounce back. It means having the strength to get through bad times to get back to a calm, peaceful, contented space. When something bad happens, you can pick yourself up, figure out what to do, and get yourself back to normal.

Resilience is about flexibility and strength. It's about stretching to deal with the problems of life and relaxing back into your usual happiness.

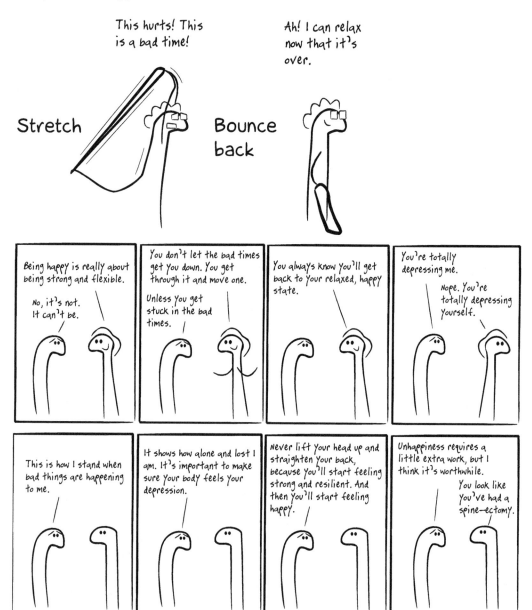

What gets in the way of resilience:

People who don't have resilience can't stay happy for very long. So what destroys their resilience?

- **Rigidity and inflexibility:** Rigid people want everything to stay the same. They can't deal with change or adapt to what's really going on. So when bad things happen, they tighten up and can't solve the problems.

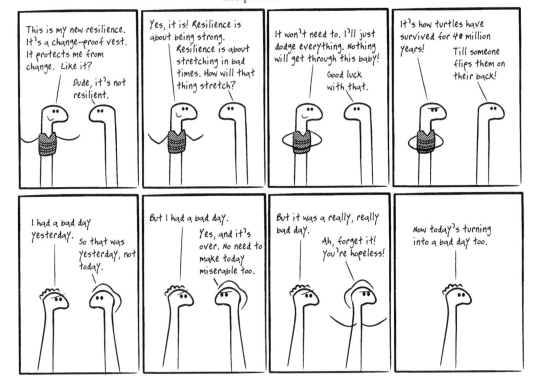

- **Perfectionism:** Perfectionists have an idea of how life is supposed to work, and they can't adapt when life works out differently. Since they believe bad things aren't "supposed to" happen to them, they get shocked and bewildered when things don't work out perfectly. The problem is not in how life works out, but in the unrealistic ideas in their brains.

People assume

... that you'll be happy in good times.
Bad times come and go.

John had mentally pictured what his
new school was going to be like. He had imagined the first day as a cheerful day of meeting new friends and getting organized. He knew it was going to be a good year!

That's why today was such a shock. Instead of meeting new friends, he was dealing with cliques and friend reunions that didn't include him, people so happy to see each other after a long summer that they didn't even notice the new student.

Meanwhile, his locker was in a faraway hallway, nowhere near his classes. And his instructors were strict and unsmiling all day.

"How's the new school?" his mom asked as the door slammed shut.

"It sucks!" John snapped. "It's not at all how I pictured it! And I never want to go back!"

- **Grudges:** A grudge is anger that you never allow to heal. You can think of it as an elastic that is pulled out but never allowed to return back to normal. Instead of dealing with your anger, you hold onto it. Grudges damage your relationships, and they get in the way of your happiness.

Which Ones are Not Resilient?

_____ Kim is unhappy because at her new school, there are different clubs than at her old school. She doesn't want to try out new clubs. She wants the same old clubs she's used to.

_____ Len is unhappy because the kid who bullied him in second grade is in his math class.

_____ Ana is unhappy because she wanted today to be perfect for the field trip. But it's raining.

You can prioritize

1 **Things that make you truly happy**
   ...are better than...

2 **Things that give you pleasure**

2. Pleasure vs. happiness

Television, movies, and ads are always telling people what happiness is. *If you buy things, you'll be happy. If you're rich and famous, you'll be happy. If you become popular, you'll be happy.*

But wealth, materialism, fame, popularity, and fun are all just one type of happiness. You can think of this kind of happiness as *pleasure*. Pleasure comes from things and other people, not from inside you.

Pleasure is great to have, but it doesn't make you happy.

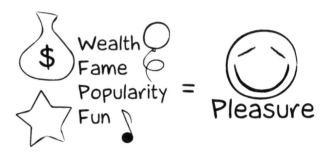

Flow happiness

There's a kind of happiness that's more reliable than plea-sure. It's called *flow happiness*. Flow happiness is reliable because it comes from inside you, not from things you have or from the people around you.

Flow happiness is always inside you. Once you find it, you can keep it going by giving it the time and energy it needs. You don't need to go out and get it anywhere.

When you're in flow, you feel peaceful, content, and very much alive. There's almost a glow inside you. Life feels meaningful and focused. Even if you're doing work, it feels like play. Instead of trying to get happiness, you let it flow out of you.

Once you find your flow happiness, you always know that you can come back to it.

What is flow happiness?

Flow happiness occurs

- when you're *completely immersed* in doing something.

- when you're doing a *task you love* or an activity that's *hard but interesting*

- when your activity requires all your *concentration*

- when you're concentrating so hard you lose *track of time* and even forget to eat

- when your activity creates a *calm energy inside* that lasts long after you stop doing it

You can prioritize

1 Things that are challenging
  ...are usually better than...

2 Things that are too easy.

Jana feels flow when she's riding

her bicycle. She loves the feel of the wind, the speed, and the straining muscles of her legs.

Paul feels flow when he's debugging an interesting problem on the computer. He focuses deeply, zeroing in on the problem, till the whole world fades away. He doesn't come back to reality until the problem is solved. Then he returns to ordinary life feeling refreshed.

Tito feels flow when he's painting and drawing. He makes time for it at least twice a week. His favorite painting place is out on one of the trails, where he can copy nature. He doesn't even see or hear the cyclists and walkers going by.

Different people experience flow doing different things.

Making happiness flow

Flow happiness doesn't happen automatically. You have to make it happen. Everybody has the ability to make their happiness flow.

How to make happiness flow:

- **Do something challenging that takes concentration:** When you do something easy, your mind gets bored. Flow happiness won't happen when you're bored. So the task has to be hard enough to make you concentrate and focus. Being lazy and choosing easy tasks won't make your happiness flow.

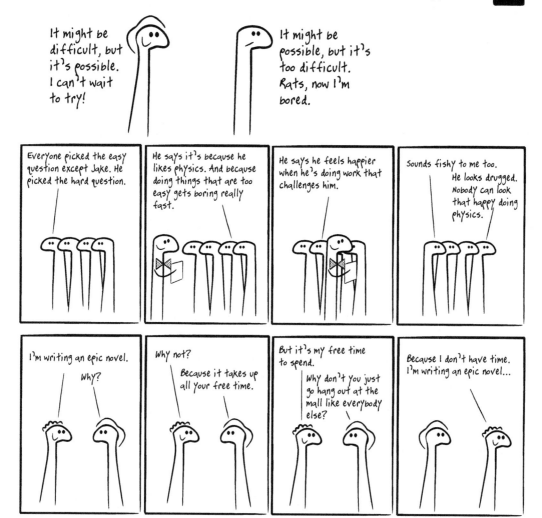

Sara loves writing. She never feels
happier than when she's writing.

Today a family friend contracted her to write a biography for a local magazine. Ssra was handed all the research but told to write it however she wanted.

Sara thought for a while and decided this was an easy project. She'd just take the research and organize it into a storyline.

But halfway through the writing, Sara was so bored, she couldn't work anymore. She felt frustrated and annoyed. She stopped working and went to do something else.

The next day, she returned to the project. But instead of trying to do it the easy way, she came up with a challenging and original way to write the bio. She became absorbed in her work till it was done.

- **Make sure it's not too frustrating:** Some activities are too hard to be challenging and interesting. If an activity is too difficult for you, then it will be frustrating. Flow activities need to be challenging, but not so hard that you can't do them.

- **Be the one in control**: When someone else is telling you what to do, it's just work. But when you are the one deciding what to do, then the activity flows out from inside you. You'll feel flow happiness when you're making the decisions.

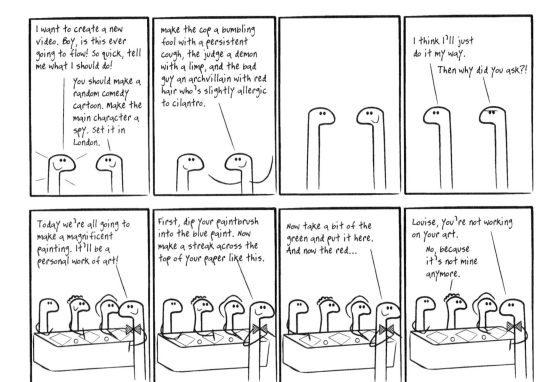

Everyone thought he was nuts.

Why would anyone want to make a career out of boxes?

But Ted loved boxes. He loved figuring out how they were designed and put together. He'd learned as much as he could about materials, how each kind works, and what it could and couldn't do. He'd spent half his childhood playing with boxes and creating his own.

Year later, nobody thought he was nuts anymore. He was the world's top consultant on box creation. He'd developed containers of every size, every style, for every purpose. His designs were considered functional works of art -- and some actually were works on art on display.

Ted's life work came from the activity that gave him flow happiness, which only gave him more flow hpapiness.

What to do

1 **Do something hard that can absorb your attention.**
Flow happiness needs concentration.

2 **Avoid excessively frustrating activities.**
Annoyance and anger get in the way of flow happiness.

3 **Stay in charge.**
Don't let others take over.

What gets in the way of flow happiness:

- **Distractions:** For flow happiness to happen, you have to be able to get right into your activity. If there are distractions, you'll lose the flow.

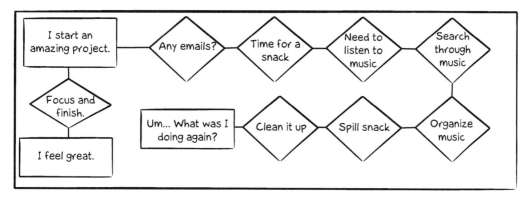

- **Fear of how you'll look to others:** Flow happiness can't happen when you're afraid of what people will think of you. You'll just end up hiding. Sure, everyone is shy when their talents and interests are out there in front of people. But be proud of yourself. When you're doing the right thing for you, you're using your talents, and most people think that's pretty cool.

I can't do this. Everyone will think I'm a dork!

The art professor put the shiny

steel object on the table.

"Is this art?" he bellowed to the class.

The students started commenting. They gave lofty explanations of how art could be made of modern materials, how art could be functional, how the smooth lines made bold statements.

Only Terry stood by silently. She felt awkward and isolated. Was she the only person who thought it wasn't art?

Suddenly, it was her turn to speak. Her throat went dry. She glanced at the professor and said in a small voice, "I don't think it's art."

The entire class whirled around to stare at her.

"Why not?" the professor asked flatly.

"Because it's too perfect," Terry continued. "It's manufactured. It has no personality. It makes no statement. It doesn't express an idea."

The other students choked, then in a rush started to argue with her.

"Wait!" the professor called, silencing them. "She's right. It's not art. In fact, it's just a chemistry lab device. Terry's the only one thinking for herself. Too much of what passes as art out there is just fads and groupthink. We need artists who can think for themselves."

Terry went on to become a famous art critic.

You can predict

1 **Do you make time for flow activities?**
If you don't, you'll start feeling grumpy or depressed.

2 **Are you afraid what other people think of you?**
If you are, you'll do the things they like instead of the things you like.

■ **Routine work taking up all your time:** Everybody has chores that they have to do every day. Happy people make sure they get their chores out of the way without dawdling and save time to do their favorite activity every day.

- **Lack of challenge:** If you have a hobby, you may have gotten into a rut of doing the same types of projects over and over again. These are too easy for you now. They don't challenge you. Soon you'll be so bored, you won't want to bother doing it anymore.

- **When you use up all your spare time on passive activities:** There's room in everyone's life for a little TV and video gaming. But these activities are passive. That means that someone else

What to do

1 **Avoid distractions.**
Give it your whole concentration.

2 **Don't be shy.**
Ignore what others think.

3 **Beware of chores.**
Get them out of the way early so they don't use up all your time.

4 **Avoid passive and easy activities.**
These just waste your time.

has planned everything out for you, and you aren't in charge. Flow happiness occurs through creative, engaging projects and activities. So if you spend all your free time on passive activities, you'll feel bored and unhappy.

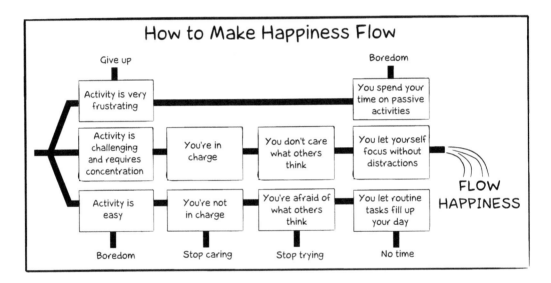

Flow happiness and serving humanity

Flow happiness can also happen when you serve humanity. Working on projects that help other people, such as charities, makes you feel good. You feel as if your actions are important.

Mia started volunteering her time

at the local seniors center. She loved writing, and she wanted to help older people write their memoires for their grandchildren.

At first, the work was very difficult. Mia knew nothing

about working with frail seniors. She also found it hard that most knew nothing about computers.

But after a few weeks, things started to flow. Her writers club became a happy place to be. The seniors loved chatting with her, and she was quickly becoming a star at the center. Most of all, Mia found she was learning a lot, on top of helping people write excellent autobiographies.

3. Moving toward better things

Another way to be happy is to make sure you're always moving toward something better. You get the bad things out of the way first so that you have the good things to look forward to.

Some people do all the fun things first and leave the hard jobs till later. But if you do that, then you're always moving toward worse things. You have nothing to look forward to. The best things are behind you, and the bad things are in front of you.

To be happy, you have to have good things to look forward to.

Get these out of the way:

So you can look forward to these:

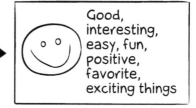

You can prioritize

1 Do the things you have
to do
..before...

2 Doing the things you want
to do.

What happens when you move toward bad things:

- **Worry and depression:** When you're always looking ahead to bad things and all the fun things are behind you, you end up worrying a lot about the future. This makes you feel depressed. But if you have all the bad things behind you, you'll have less to worry about. You'll look forward to your future instead of dreading it.

- **Stress:** Putting off the annoying tasks till later creates stress in your life. It turns simple problems into bigger problems because you don't deal with them in time. Besides, you know those bothersome tasks are still ahead of you. Instead of putting things off, get the work out of the way as soon as possible. Then you'll have less stress and lots of free time to do the things you love.

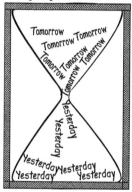

Lisa was dreading doing her research

report all week. She kept putting it off because it was making her feel stressed and worried.

"Get started soon," her roommate warned. "It takes forever."

Mia decided that was good advice. So reluctantly, she placed the report instructions in the middle of her deak.

The day before the deadline, Mia still had nothing written.

"But I started days ago!" she wailed.

"What did you do?" her roommate asked.

"I spent a long time designing a beautiful cover. And I went for long walks to think about the report. And I surfed the internet a little."

"So basically, you did just easy, unimportant things and left the real work till later. You wanted to avoid stress and worry, but you ended up making it worse by trying to run away from it."

You can predict

1 Do you get chores out of the way as soon as possible?
If you do, you'll always be happy about what's ahead.

2 Do you procrastinate?
If you do, you'll get more and more stressed as your deadline approaches.

- **Long-term problems:** When you do all the fun things now and leave the hard work for later, you trade short-term pleasure for long-term pain. That means you'll always be heading into problems. To be happy, you need to work on creating happiness for the future, since that's where you're headed.

Tips for moving into better things:

- **Save the best for last:** Get the worst tasks out of the way first. Then work on the next-worst ones. Even though you're doing the jobs you dislike the most, you'll find you feel happier and happier—because those jobs are out of the way. Eventually, you'll have only your favorites ahead of you.

- **Remove bad things from your future.** It may feel good to avoid the things you dislike, but they don't go away, and you'll have to face them eventually. Stay in control of the things you dislike. Remove them from your future, and put them in your past.

■ **Set aside time for flow activities.** You'll be happiest if you have time for the creative, engaging, challenging activities that give you flow happiness. You don't want worries about all the chores and homework you haven't done to ruin your flow activity time.

Which Ones Move into Better Things?

_____ Jenny wants to buy a new sofa. So she saves up her money till she can afford to buy one.

_____ Lois wants to buy a new table. So she runs down to the store and buys one on her credit card. She'll pay for it later.

_____ Ed loves designing websites. At his job today, he has to get three reports done and design one website. He decides to leave the website till last.

_____ For homework, Max has to read a fun novel and finish two pages of very tedious math. He decides to read the novel first.

_____ Susie knows she needs some exercise. So she schedules it for the mornings. She knows that if she schedules it for the evenings, something more fun will come up, and she won't do it.

---

4. Pessimism

Pessimism is a pattern of thinking that focuses on the bad, not on the good. Pessimists see only bad things. They believe taht everything is getting worse, not better. So they're never happy.

Pessimism comes from false explanation patterns in the pessimist's brain. No matter what the input, the output will always be a sad thought.

Input   Output

Pessimistic Explanations

Pessimism comes from pessimistic explanation patterns. These explanation patterns are illogical. They lead you to false conclusions. But because you're not thinking clearly, you believe them.

Depressing explanation patterns

A depressing explanation finds the most depressing conclusion, no matter waht. It makes you explain away the good things and blame yourself for the bad things. It also makes you blind to the evidence that your conclusions are wrong.

- **When good things happen to you:** When good things happen to you, you tell yourself that it was *not* because of you or anything you did. It was because of *something else.*

"This painting is excellent, Ed!" the teacher exclaimed, holding up his art.

"No, it isn't," Ed said. "It sucks."

"Really. It's fantastic. You should enter it in the regional contest."

"There's no point. I'd never win. Not with that piece of crap."

"I'm really encouraging you to enter," the teacher repeated. "This painting is creative and original."

"I hate it. It just happened by accident. I'm no artist."

"Well, I'm saying you are. And there's no such thing as accidents in art."

"Well, listen to me. It's a fluke. I'm no artist. One fluke doesn't count for anything."

The teacher stared at him. "Can't you even hear what I'm saying? Or have you already decided you're a loser?"

"Oh, I'm a loser all right. And I'm not going to enter that contest because I don't want to waste my time. Or anybody else's time."

The teacher just sighed and gave up.

- **When bad things happen to you:** When bad things happen to you, you tell yourself it's because of *you*. You ignore anything else that might have contributed to the problem. You picture yourself forever moving into worse and worse things. This ensures that you always feel bad.

Spotting a pessimistic explanation

One way to spot pessimistic explanation patterns is to look for negative words. Pessimistic explanations all sound the same because they use the same words.

- **"Forever" words:** Pessimistic explanations explain bad things with *forever* words like *never, always*. They conclude that the problems are permanent and will never go away. But of course, nothing in life is permanent, so these *forever* words are false.

I'm always wrong! I never get things right! It's always going to be this way!

- **"Everywhere/everyone" words:** Pessimistic explanations explain bad things with *everywhere/ everyone* words like *everywhere, nowhere, everybody, nobody.* They conclude that the problems are inescapable, and everybody knows it. But of course, all problems have solutions, and all people have different opinions, so these *every- where/everyone* words are false.

Everyone hates me! Nobody ever calls me!

- **Insult words:** Pessimistic expla- nations use insult words like *stupid, loser, lousy, hopeless.* Anger and sadness blind you to your talents and skills and make you stop believing in them.

I'm a stupid dumdum head!

What to do

1 Watch for *forever* words
Nothing is forever.

2 Watch for *everywhere/ everyone* words.
These are exaggerations.

3 Watch for insult words.
Self-insults come from emotions, not from facts.

4 Listen to others.
They may be trying to help you.

Life sucks. I'll never lose weight. Good things never last.

I never know what to do. I'll be stuck in this lousy job forever. Everybody knows I'm a loser.

I haven't got a chance, so why bother trying? I never win. Nobody cares if I go or not.

You're just having a bad day.

So what else is new?

- **Arguments:** Your friends and family try to help you find more realistic explanations, but your pessi- mistic explanations won't let you listen. You believe they're deluded and shut them out. This makes you feel lonely as well as unhappy.

I don't do anything right. I'm a screw-up. And don't try any of your Jedi mind tricks to convince me I'm not!

Okay.

Okay?! What do you mean "okay"?! You always argue with me when I say I'm a loser!

Well, maybe this time you're right.

Right?! How can I be right all of a sudden? Either I'm a loser or I'm not!

Well, are you?

What kind of a question is that? Of course not! You're the one always telling me what I'm good at! Jeesh!

I sense a disturbance in the Force.

Giggle.

Spot the Pessimistic Explanations

_____ I lost because I didn't train hard enough. Also, the other runners are older and bigger than me. I need to train more and enter the right race.

_____ I lost because I'm no good. I never do anything right. I'm always last. It's always been this way, ever since I can remember.

_____ I won because of a fluke. The other runners were all smaller than me. it wasn't because I'm any good.

_____ I won because I ran a great race. All that training has paid off.

_____ I never win and I probably never will. The coach always places me in easy races because she feels sorry for me.

Realistic explanations

Realistic explanations are the opposite of pessimistic explanations. People who are realistic are happier than people who are pessimistic.

To be realistic, look for facts before you make conclusions. Place blame only where there's evidence that the blame belongs there. Stay logical and look for solutions, rather than being emotional and getting stuck in the problems.

Realistic explanation patterns

- **When good things happen to you:** When good things happen to you, you recognize that at least part of the good outcome was because of you and the things you did.

■ **When bad things happen to you:** When bad things happen to you, you consider the context. You don't just blame yourself, especially for events that weren't your fault. You also look for solutions so that you picture yourself moving into better things. Basically, when problems occur, you look for the real-life reasons why they happened and search practical ways to solve them.

Spotting a realistic explanation

■ **"Sometimes" words:** Realistic explanations explain bad things with *sometimes* words like *today, this month, this time*. They conclude that your problems are temporary and will go away, especially if you make changes.

■ **"Somewhere/someone" words:** Realistic explanations explain bad things with *somewhere/ someone* words like *this group, he, she, this situation*. They recognize that at least part of the problem is related to the context. It also recognizes that the problem is limited.

The girls in that clique don't like me. But that doesn't mean nobody likes me. I'm not a loser. I have other friends. I'm sad and angry about it, but I don't really want to be in a clique anyway.

■ **Emotion words:** Realistic explanations use emotion words like *sad, disappointed, concerned*, rather than insult words like *loser, stupid*. They help you think about your emotions as feelings, not as explanations.

■ **Solution talk:** Instead of focusing on the problems, realistic explanations focus on the solutions. They help you consider ways to fix the problems. You picture yourself moving toward better things.

I probably need a new strategy. I also need some advice on what to do differently.

What to do

1 Use *sometimes* words
  Problems are temporary.

2 Use *somewhere/someone* words.
  Problems are limited.

3 Use emotion words.
  Identify how you're feeling.

4 Talk about solutions.
  Focus on solving the problem.

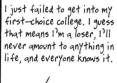

Ron stared at his artwork from across

the room as he strode over to it. There was something attached to the side. As he reached it, he realized it was a first-prize ribbon.

He blinked a few times, fingering the ribbon. He hadn't even bothered to go to the awards ceremony because he was so certain his art was the worst in the show. It didn't look like anyone else's. It stood out like a sore thumb.

The adjudicators' comments were pinned to the wall beside the canvas. He scanned them: "... original vision ... refreshing .... eye-catching ... eloquent..."

The voices in his head were getting louder: "Of course, they don't mean it. It was a fluke. Nobody likes your art. It's ugly. You'll never be any good."

But Ron brushed those voices away and reread the adjudicators' comments. These were the experts. And if they said he was good, then it made a lot of sense to believe them.

Tips for controlling pessimistic explanations:

- **Identify your emotions:** Anxiety, fear of change, embarrassment, and disappointment are at the heart of pessimistic explanations. Ask yourself what emotions you're feeling. Once you've recognized your emotions, they'll be less powerful, and you'll have a better chance of coming up with realistic explanations.

- **Picture yourself moving into better things:** To be happy, you need to see yourself moving into a happier future. Whatever the problems are today, imagine solving them and moving on. Instead of picturing endless misery, think about what you can change to get where you want to go.

- **Never say "never":** It's pompous to say *never*. Who's expert enough to predict the future? Nobody is. The past is no indication of what the future will be. Whenever you make predictions about the future using *forever* words, stop yourself and question your logic.

- **Accept change:** Problems go away when you fix them. This means changing the way you do things. Often change is good and leads to better things. But you have to accept the need for change first.

What to do

1 **Figure out how you feel.**
   Don't let emotions do your thinking.

2 **Imagine a good future.**
   Picture moving into better things.

3 **Avoid saying *never*.**
   You can't predict the future.

4 **Accept change.**
   Solving problems involves change.

5 **Imagine if someone else said it.**
   Don't let the voice inside your head insult you.

- **Imagine if someone else said it:** When you're in a bad mood, a negative voice inside your head can start growling insults at you. Instead of listening to that voice, imagine that someone else said those things to you. Would you argue? Would you fight back? Do the same for the negative voice inside your head.

Voice in your head	If someone else said it
Nobody ever likes me. So nobody is going to like me at this party. I'm not going to have fun, so I might as well go home now.	Nobody ever likes you. So nobody is going to like you at this party. You're not going to have fun, so you might as well go home now. Hold it right there, buster! Those aren't facts! I have friends! And I'm going to stay, so take your dumb ideas to someone who'll listen.

Pessmistic (P) or Realistic (R)?

_____ This has been a terrible day! But I'll fix some of these mistakes, and things will turn around by tomorrow.

_____ This has been the worst day ever! I humiliated myself in front of everyone! And I can tell it's never going to get any better.

_____ This problem is huge. I'm scared of it because to solve it, I have to change my usual way of doing things. Change makes me nervous.

_____ This problem is huge. I can never solve it. It's just going to follow me now for the rest of my life.

_____ I feel so embarrassed I want to crawl away and hide. But that doesn't mean that this problem can't be solved. I have to somehow get past my emotions.

Summary

Happiness is like an elastic band. It pulls and stretches during bad times but relaxes back to the normal state when the bad times are over.

Happiness starts with resilience. Resilience is strength and flexibility. When you're resilient, you stretch through bad times and come out fine at the other side.

Happiness is not the same as pleasure. Money, fun, and popularity are types of pleasure, and they can't make people happy for long. A deeper kind of happiness—often called *flow happiness*—comes from doing the things you love. True happiness can also come from serving humanity.

One way to make yourself happy is to plan your life so that

you're always moving from bad things into good things. Get tedious, time-consuming, and dislikable tasks out of the way first so that you always have fun, relaxing, and interesting tasks ahead of you.

Finally, to be happy, you need to get control of pessimistic thinking patterns. Pessimistic thoughts aren't realistic or logical. They come from our emotions. Realistic thinking patterns look for solutions.

Suggested Answers to Quiz Boxes

page 10: She expected you would pay attention to her silent communication and take her home. He assumed that you ate and talked a lot on purpose, trying to be rude and self-centered.

page 11: 2, 1; 1, 2; 1, 2; 1, 2

page 16: 2nd

page 23: 1st, 2nd

page 25: 1st, 2nd, possibly 3rd

page 28: 2nd, 3rd

page 38: open to adventure, wary of adventure; introvert, extrovert; emotional sensitivity

page 42: true, false, false, false

page 45: 1st, 2nd

page 46: 1st, 3rd, 4th

page 49: 1st, 3rd, 5th, 7th

page 51: 1st, 2nd, 4th

page 55: All except the last one.

page 57: outer, inner, inner, outer, inner, outer

page 59: 1st, 3rd, 4th, 6th, 7th

page 62: 1st, 3rd

page 65: 1st, 3rds

page 72: 2nd, 4th, 5th not really, 6th not necessarily

page 76: All except the last one

page 83: All except the first one

page 87: 1st, 2nd, 5th

page 93: bored, interested, bored, bored, interested, interested

page 98: 5, 1-2, 2, 4, 3-4, 1-2, 1-2, 3 (Answers will vary)

page 103: 2nd, 4th

pagea 105: over, under; under, over; under, over

page 107: Answers will vary

page 109: Answers will vary

page 116: Answers will vary

page 127: attention/hunger/tiredness; love

page 131: He's angry. The other man was trying to rob him. It was an accident. It's part of a practical joke. They're street comedians. The man is a criminal getting revenge on the man who turned him in 20 years ago. (Answers will vary.)

pagae 133: They might assume that you agree.

page 138: 1st, 3rd, 4th, 5th

page 147: C, A, D, B

page 152: C, A, D, B

page 158: D, B, F, D

page 161: Answers will vary.

page 169: All

page 183: 1st, 3rd, 5th

page 188: 2nd, 3rd, 5th

page 193: R, P, R, P, R

CPSIA information can be obtained
at www.ICGtesting.com
Printed in the USA
LVOW02s1654150616

492731LV00007B/149/P